MIND BLOWING MATHS

MIND
BLOWING
MATHS

Written by
Lisa Regan

Illustrated by
Rhys Jefferys

ARCTURUS

ARCTURUS

This edition published in 2018 by Arcturus Publishing Limited
26/27 Bickels Yard, 151–153 Bermondsey Street,
London SE1 3HA, UK

Illustrated by Rhys Jefferys
Written by Lisa Regan
Edited by Becca Clunes and Donna Gregory
Designed by Square and Circus

ISBN: 978-1-78828-608-4
CH006208NT
Supplier 26 Date 1118 Print run 6839

Printed in China

What is STEM?

STEM is a world-wide initiative that aims to cultivate an interest in
Science, Technology, Engineering, and Mathematics, in an effort to
promote these disciplines to as wide a variety of students as possible.

Contents

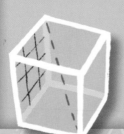

It all adds up!

It's not uncommon to hear people moan about math—What use is it? Why do I need it? But a moment's thought will reveal that you need basic number skills for so many things in life. They help you handle your money, share things fairly, and do practical tasks like building things, decorating your room, or working out how far you have run. If you throw yourself into geometry and algebra, you'll soon realize that it's fun!

Without mathematicians, we wouldn't have sent people into space, or have seen photographs of distant planets, or even be able to fly around the world in a plane. Our days would be spent without computers and phones, and with no gaming or knowledge of what's trending on social media. Mathematical thinkers have posed and answered some of the greatest questions in history that have led to the development of humankind. When you learn to think in a mathematical way, the possibilities are infinite; you really could be the next person to change the world. How about it?

ALL SORTS OF NUMBERS

Counting on our fingers is primitive, but effective. It seems an instinctive way to count to ten, although in some cultures people are more likely to use their fingers to count to twelve, or even twenty. Try it—use your thumb as a pointer and touch it on each knuckle (or finger bone) of each finger on one hand. 1 to 12, see?

Through time, humans have developed ways to translate counting into a written form. It allows us to make much bigger numbers, keep records, and show the concept of zero. It also paved the way for keeping accounts, working out equations, and going below zero into negative numbers. There really are all sorts of numbers out there!

Zero is the youngest of all the numbers—and not just because it comes before 1, 2, and 3. The symbol didn't even exist in Europe until after the twelfth century, and in medieval Italy, it was illegal to use a 0!

Counting to ten

Counting may seem as easy as 1, 2, 3, but that all depends on where you live, and what you need to count. While our culture counts hundreds, thousands, millions, and more, some societies have far fewer numbers.

CROSS-CULTURAL

Small numbers are easy to visualize. If you placed four books on a table, you would instinctively know how many were there. If you upped the number to 64, however, it would be much harder to judge the quantity quickly. Certain cultures don't even have words for numbers over four or five; they simply have a word for "many" or "big." In remote villages where people don't use money, or own things, life can be lived entirely without numbers.

Zoologists have found that some other animals, including rhesus monkeys and bees, can also tell the difference between the number of items in small groups of objects.

COUNT ON ME

An easy way to count is to use your fingers and thumbs. Our counting is based around the number ten for exactly that reason. (If we all had only one hand, we would probably count in fives.) Our system is called the decimal system, or base 10, and has ten digits (0, 1, 2, 3, 4, 5, 6, 7, 8, 9). When you reach 9, and run out of digits, you add a new column on the left to give more options. That way, 14 represents 1 lot of ten and 4 ones.

Counting in base 5 gives us: 1, 2, 3, 4, 10, 11, 12, 13, 14, 20, 21 and so on. 10 is 1 five and 0 ones, 22 is 2 fives and 2 ones (so, 5 and 12 respectively).

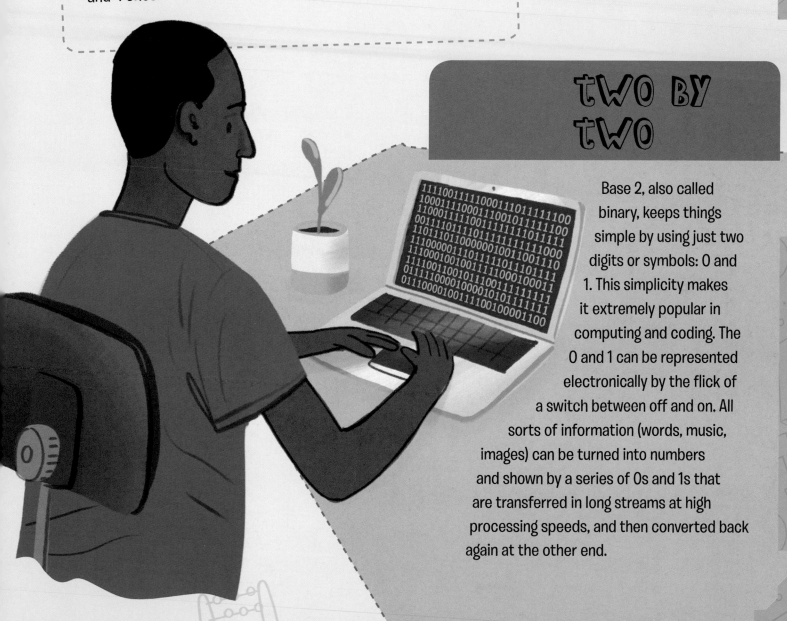

TWO BY TWO

Base 2, also called binary, keeps things simple by using just two digits or symbols: 0 and 1. This simplicity makes it extremely popular in computing and coding. The 0 and 1 can be represented electronically by the flick of a switch between off and on. All sorts of information (words, music, images) can be turned into numbers and shown by a series of 0s and 1s that are transferred in long streams at high processing speeds, and then converted back again at the other end.

Show and tell

You might think that numbers are as old as humans themselves, but cavemen didn't need to count. It was only when early civilizations settled and began building and trading that numbers became really useful tools. Even then, they weren't written in the way you write them today.

THE TEST OF TIME

The Sumerians also invented or developed the wheel, writing, farming, bronze, irrigation canals, and sailing boats.

The first counting was done with tally marks on sticks, bones, or clay. Five marks meant you owned five cows, or five bags of grain. The Sumerians (who lived between around 5,000 BCE and 1,000 CE in what is now Iraq) developed a kind of picture-writing called cuneiform to record numbers. Their symbols were based around a Y shape, and made up a base-60 system that is still used today for measuring time and angles (that's why there are 60 minutes in an hour).

PLACE VALUE

Cuneiform, like the decimal system, is a place-value system, where the position of the symbols shows their value. In base 10, each number is ten times the value of the number to the right of it. For example, 1954 is made up of 1 thousand, 9 hundreds, 5 tens, and 4 units or ones. The Romans used letters instead of numbers, but they were non-positional. A Roman V means five wherever it appears, not fifty or five hundred.

The numerals 1 to 9 were introduced to Europe by the Italian mathematician Leonardo of Pisa, better known as Fibonacci.

SMALLER AND BETTER

The numerals you use today are known as Hindu-Arabic and were first devised in India. People in that country started using them in around 500 CE. A different symbol is used for each number from one to nine. This means that really big numbers can be shown with far fewer symbols than other systems. Hindu-Arabic numerals also opened the door to much more complicated mathematical processes, from fractions and equations to algebra and geometry.

From zero to hero

Imagine life without zero. It would be like ... well, nothing you can imagine! And yet there was no zero symbol until around the seventh century, when those clever Indian mathematicians saw there was a zero-shaped hole that needed filling.

THE ABSENCE OF ZERO

Early cultures counted on an abacus, moving beads in rows to carry out calculations. The idea of zero was familiar; if you owned a dozen bags of rice and sold them all, you had none left. If you sold two of them, it left an empty column on your abacus. Mathematicians wanted a written system that could show this, and began using a dot as a placeholder. This dot became the 0 that we use today, although it was only introduced to Europe in the twelfth century.

NOW IT'S A NUMBER

The concept of zero as an actual number, not just a place holder, was also developed by Indian mathematicians. In the seventh century, Brahmagupta wrote about adding and subtracting and multiplying by 0. Now, you know that multiplying anything by zero gives you zero. No matter what numbers are involved, it is always zero. So $987 \times 0 = 0$ and $987 \times 654 \times 321 \times 0 = 0$. Brahmagupta is credited as the first person to set that out for everyone to understand.

There was no Year Zero! The Western calendar went straight from 1 BCE to 1 CE.

ZERO COUNTS

Zero as a number is so important because it sits between positive and negative numbers. Negative numbers are hard to imagine. If you own 4 cows you can only sell 4 cows, no more. You cannot have a minus number of cows. Yet again, Brahmagupta showed his genius by setting out rules for this difficult idea, describing them as "debts" in contrast to positive numbers which are "fortunes." It was many centuries before the Western world came to terms with this idea.

WOW! (times a million)

If we only needed to count cows in a field, numbers wouldn't need to be particularly big. But as human society has become more complicated, and we have found out more about the world around us, we need bigger and bigger numbers and increasingly clever ways to write them.

$$1000000000000000000000$$

BIG QUESTIONS

How many stars are there in the universe? How many cells are there in the human body? Answers to questions like these require gigantic numbers, with so many zeroes they become hard to write down. Mathematicians express such large numbers using powers of 10. This is when the number 10 is multiplied over and over again. So $10^2 = 10 \times 10 = 100$, and $10^3 = 10 \times 10 \times 10 = 1,000$. To express different numbers with lots of zeros, we multiply them by these powers of 10. So, 5,000 is equal to 5×10^3, or $5 \times 10 \times 10 \times 10$.

Based on the Hubble Space Telescope's observations, there are around 100 billion galaxies, and an average of 100 billion stars in each, so there may be over 10^{22} stars out there.

In 2009, Zimbabwe's inflation was so high it printed a 100 trillion dollar note (which was just enough to buy a loaf of bread).

The base number (the 10 in 10^3, for example) does not have to be a whole number (called an integer). Huge numbers, such as the number of cells in the human body, don't always work so neatly. A single digit, with decimal places if needed, reduces any giant number to a manageable size. The small number (the power) after the ten tells us how many places to move the decimal point to the right, filling the gaps with zeroes. (In case you were wondering, there are estimated to be 3.72×10^{13} cells (37.2 trillion) in the human body.)

THE NAME GAME

Like small numbers, big numbers need names so we can discuss them. It is much easier to talk about a million than a thousand thousand (both are 1 with six zeroes after it). A billion is a thousand million, and a trillion is a million million. In 1920, the mathematician Edward Kasner decided a name was needed for a number with 100 zeroes (10^{100}) and his 9-year-old nephew made up the name googol. It is a phenomenally huge number, far bigger than the number of stars in the universe.

To infinity and beyond!

The idea of infinity is used to describe a number (or amount) that is not enormous—it is endless. Our minds find it very difficult to cope with the thought of something going on and on and on and on ... So, don't worry if this makes your brain hurt!

KEEP COUNTING

Infinity may have no end, but it comes in different sizes. Georg Cantor (1845–1918) proposed that some infinite sets are "small" and countable while others are "large" and uncountable. If you had an infinite number of books, you could still begin to count them: 1, 2, 3, 4, and so on. An uncountable infinity is too big to even begin. Think about the decimals in between the numbers 1 and 2. There are an infinite amount—and that's just between two whole numbers. There are also an infinite amount of decimals in between 1.1 and 1.2, and 1.11 and 1.12. Yikes!

MONKEY MAGIC

Because infinity has no end, anything is possible (although not probable—that's different). To illustrate this, mathematicians such as Émile Borel (1871–1956) invented the Monkey Metaphor. Imagine a monkey typing on a laptop. Given an infinite amount of time, the monkey will at some point type a great work of literature such as Shakespeare's *Hamlet*. The chances are extremely low, but they're higher than zero, which is good enough for a mathematician.

BRAIN BOGGLING

German mathematician David Hilbert (1862–1943) created a "thought experiment" to show how countable infinities work. Imagine a hotel with an infinite number of rooms. Each room is occupied (so, total number of guests = ∞). One more person arrives; can they get a room? Yes! Everyone moves up one room and the visitor manages to stay: ∞ + 1 = ∞. Even if an infinite number of people turn up, they can still stay. All the current guests move into a room number 2 x their current room number, so they are all in even numbered rooms. The infinite number of odd rooms are now all free and so the infinite number of guests can stay the night too: ∞ + ∞ = ∞.

Don't be so negative!

Numbers don't simply start at zero and count up. You can count below zero, too, with negative numbers. They often confuse people, but they're easy to see on a number line. The further left you go, the smaller the number.

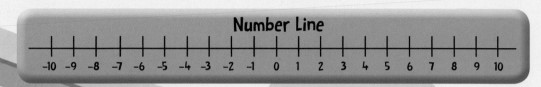

Number Line

-10 -9 -8 -7 -6 -5 -4 -3 -2 -1 0 1 2 3 4 5 6 7 8 9 10

−4 is less than 4.

REALLY NEGATIVE

You might think that negative numbers are hard to understand because they don't occur in real life. (Remember, you can't have a minus number of cows? See page 13.) Except—they can, and they do. An elevator that visits underground floors uses minus numbers to get you there. A person who spends more money than is in their account goes overdrawn, which is a minus amount. One of the most clearly visible examples is a thermometer, which shows temperatures less than zero when it drops below freezing point.

MONEY MATTERS

Chinese mathematicians were the first to use negative numbers, way back in 200 BCE. They used them when counting money. Any money earned was positive, and shown in red on their number rod system. Any money spent was negative and shown in black. They recognized that more money could be spent than earned. Interestingly, your bank account uses red and black in the opposite way. If you're "in the red" it means you have minus money!

the lowest theoretical temperature is –273°C (–459°F), called absolute zero. It corresponds to 0 Kelvin. Even scientists avoid using negative numbers where they can!

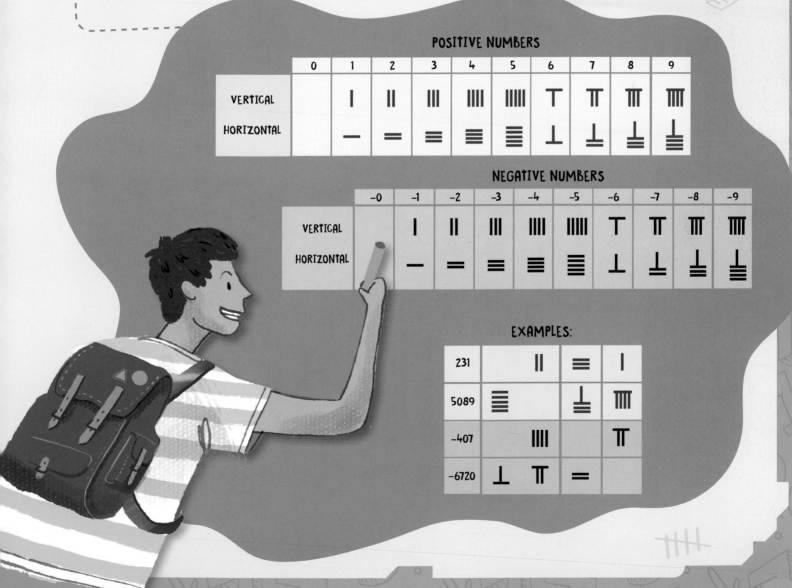

POSITIVE NUMBERS

	0	1	2	3	4	5	6	7	8	9
VERTICAL		I	II	III	IIII	IIIII	⊤	⊤⊤	⊤⊤⊤	⊤⊤⊤⊤
HORIZONTAL		—	=	≡	≣	≣	⊥	⊥	⊥	⊥

NEGATIVE NUMBERS

	–0	–1	–2	–3	–4	–5	–6	–7	–8	–9
VERTICAL		I	II	III	IIII	IIIII	⊤	⊤⊤	⊤⊤⊤	⊤⊤⊤⊤
HORIZONTAL		—	=	≡	≣	≣	⊥	⊥	⊥	⊥

EXAMPLES:

231	II	=	I
5089	≡	⊥	⊤⊤⊤⊤
–407	IIII		⊤⊤
–6720	⊥	⊤⊤	=

In their prime

Prime numbers are special, and important. They are positive, whole numbers that have only two factors, themselves and 1. They help mathematicians understand all sorts of things about the structure of numbers.

SIMPLE SIEVE

How do you work out which numbers are prime? You use a sieve! A prime sieve is an algorithm (a set of rules) for finding prime numbers. In around 250 BCE the Greek mathematician Eratosthenes designed a sieve so simple that anyone can use it. An example is shown here, for all primes up to 100, but it works up to 500, 10,000 or any number you choose.

How it works:

Begin by crossing out the number 1. It is not a prime number as it does not have two factors. Now, circle the first unmarked number: 2. Cross out all of its multiples. Circle the next unmarked number: 3. Its first multiple, 6, is already crossed out. Jump to 3 x 3 (9) and cross out all remaining multiples. The next unmarked number is 5. Cross out its first unmarked multiple: 5 × 5 (25). Continue like this until the first unmarked multiple is greater than 100.

All primes are greater than 1, so strike it through immediately.

A number that isn't prime is composite—that is, made by multiplying two smaller whole numbers (other than 1).

1̶	②	③	4̶	⑤	6̶	⑦	8̶	9̶	1̶0̶
⑪	12	⑬	1̶4̶	1̶5̶	1̶6̶	⑰	1̶8̶	⑲	2̶0̶
2̶1̶	22	㉓	24	25	26	27	28	㉙	30
㉛	3̶2̶	33	34	35	36	3̶7̶	3̶8̶	3̶9̶	40
㊶	42	㊸	44	45	46	47	48	49	50
5̶1̶	52	㊿	54	55	56	57	58	㊾	60
㉑	62	63	64	65	66	㊿	68	69	7̶0̶
㉗	72	㉝	7̶4̶	75	76	77	78	㉙	80
8̶1̶	82	㊳	84	85	8̶6̶	87	88	㊟	90
9̶1̶	92	93	94	95	96	㊼	98	9̶9̶	1̶0̶0̶

PRIMES AND PATTERNS

Numbers can be arranged in rows and columns known as arrays. The number 12 can be shown as 2 rows of 6 or 3 rows of 4. A prime number makes only one array. The number 7 is a row of 7, nothing else. While we're multiplying, here's another thing about prime numbers—every number greater than 1 can be written as a product of primes. For example, 24 = 3 x 2 x 2 x 2.

PRIME	COMPOSITE
2	
3	
	4
5	
	6
7	
	8
	9
	10
11	
	12

SAFETY IN NUMBERS

Finding out which prime numbers multiply together to make a huge number is a slow, difficult process, even for a computer. It can take years or even centuries of trial and error. Encryption systems use prime factoring to keep details (such as your bank account or streaming subscription) safe from hackers and thieves. The product of two primes is used to encrypt a message, and the hard-to-figure primes are needed to decrypt it and access the information.

All by myself

If you multiply a whole number by itself, it forms a square. It can be shown in a square array (see page 21), and is called a square number, a perfect square, or just a square. Numbers can form triangles, too, which can be added to make squares.

Square numbers end only in 1, 4, 6, 9, 00 or 25.

FAIR AND SQUARE

A square number is shown as n x n or n^2. The first square number is 1, because 1 x 1 = 1. The first triangular number is also 1. To make the next triangular number, add 2 dots beneath to form a triangle (1 + 2 = 3). Triangular numbers are simply the sum of consecutive numbers (e.g., 1 + 2 + 3 + 4 + 5 = 15). Keep adding rows of dots, or use the formula $x_n = n(n+1)/2$. For example, to find the 5th triangular number, substitute the n: $x_5 = 5(5+1)/2 = 15$.

NUMBER THEORY

1 + 3 = 4

3 + 6 = 9

6 + 10 = 16

The sum of any two consecutive triangular numbers is always a square number. You can see this if you twist the triangles and slot them together. It sounds complicated, but it is easy to see if you draw it (left). The study of relationships of positive integers (whole numbers) is known as number theory. It was of particular interest to German mathematician Carl Gauss who discovered in 1796 that every integer can be made by adding together a maximum of three triangular numbers.

← ONES

← COUNTING NUMBERS

← TRIANGULAR NUMBERS

```
              1
           1     1
        1     2     1
     1     3     3     1
  1     4     6     4     1
1     5    10    10     5     1
1   6    15    20    15    6    1
1  7   21   35   35   21   7   1
```

TRIANGULAR THINKING

The seventeeth-century French mathematician Blaise Pascal (1623–1662, left) gave his name to a fascinating number theory triangle. Add together any two numbers and you get the number directly below. Add up the numbers on each horizontal row and they double each time. Look down the third diagonal and you can see all the triangular numbers. Pascal's triangle displays all sorts of patterns and probability outcomes (too many to mention here!).

4 April 2016 was a square root day: 4/4/16. The next one will be 5 May 2025 (5/5/25). Can you work out the one after that?

IT'S A CLASSIC

Mathematicians love to set and solve problems, often using real-life situations to help make them easier to understand. Let's take a look at a pirate problem (sometimes called the jail-break problem).

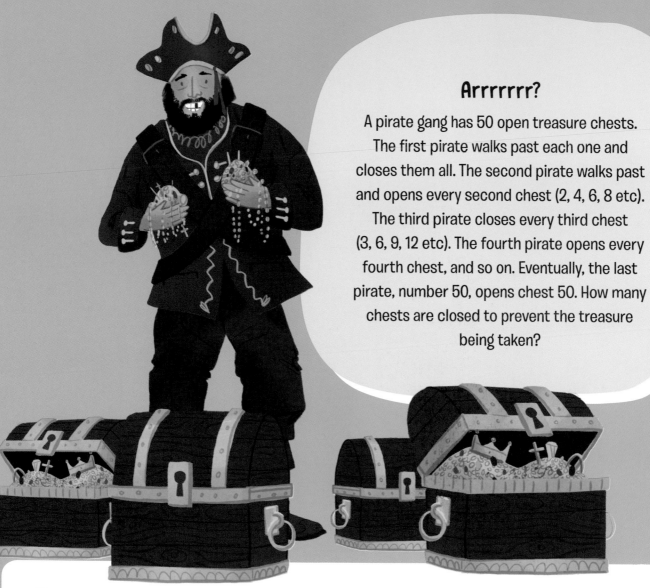

Arrrrrrr?

A pirate gang has 50 open treasure chests. The first pirate walks past each one and closes them all. The second pirate walks past and opens every second chest (2, 4, 6, 8 etc). The third pirate closes every third chest (3, 6, 9, 12 etc). The fourth pirate opens every fourth chest, and so on. Eventually, the last pirate, number 50, opens chest 50. How many chests are closed to prevent the treasure being taken?

Aharrrrrr!

Only chests 1, 4, 9, 16, 25, 36, and 49 are closed. Notice the pattern (+3, +5, +7, +9) but also the important thing—they are all square numbers.

Each chest is visited only by its factors—for example, chest 10 is visited by pirates 1, 2, 5, and 10.

That means it is changed four times (closed, opened, closed, opened). Any chest with an even number of factors ends up open. The only chests with an odd number of factors are square numbers. Why? Because here, a number is multiplied by itself (6 x 6 = 36) so pirate 6 visits it a single time.

LET'S GET
GEOMETRIC

Shapes are everywhere. They are one of the first things you learn about when you trace a triangle, shade in a square, or draw circular wheels on a car. An understanding of shapes is vital for the more complex tasks of building, map-making, and getting us from place to place (whether those places are your home and your school, or a rocket launch pad and the Moon).

Geometry can help us to look around a corner, make a den, buy the right amount of paint to decorate a room, or work out how much pizza you've eaten. This type of mathematics began in Ancient Egypt more than 5,000 years ago, and without it, there would be no medical scanning machines, no trains, and no video games. Imagine that!

A two-dimensional shape with straight sides is called a polygon. Polygons literally come in all shapes and sizes. One with 13 sides is called a triskaidecagon, or just a 13-gon for ease. A polygon with 1,000 sides is called a chiliagon.

All the threes

A triangle has three angles and three sides. Satisfyingly, there are three types of triangle, too! These are equilateral, isosceles, and scalene. The three angles inside a triangle always add up to the same number: 180 degrees.

Equilateral   Isosceles   Scalene

TRIANGULATION STATION

If you've ever spotted construction workers peering through a viewfinder on top of a tripod, you have seen triangulation in action. They are measuring angles and distances with great accuracy to map out the area. The special relationship between angles and sides of a triangle means that, if we know two angles to a fixed point somewhere in the distance, we can work out how far away it is. We can slowly build up a map of the land by drawing triangles all over it.

A "right triangle" has one right angle of 90°. A triangle with one angle larger than 90° is known as "oblique." A triangle with all angles smaller than 90° is called "acute."

PRETTY POLY

A polygon is a shape made from straight sides. The least number of possible sides is three. The study of the relationship between angles and sides of a triangle is known as trigonometry. Using known angles and sides allows us to calculate unknown angles and sides. That knowledge can be put to practical use in map-making, navigation, geology, astronomy, and when launching spacecraft.

triangulation can be used to pinpoint disasters such as earthquakes and forest fires.

ALL AT SEA

Thales (*c.*624 BCE–546 BCE), a philosopher often said to be the father of mathematics in Ancient Greece, used triangles to solve a tricky measurement problem—how far from shore was a ship? Long distances were often measured by stretching a rope or chain between two points. This was clearly impossible across the water, but Thales proposed that two people on shore, at a known distance apart, could measure the angles from their position to the boat, and then work out the distance to the boat.

Bouncing back

An angle is formed where two lines meet at a point. They can affect you without you even being aware of it. A little angle know-how can help you win at pool or mini golf, or mess with your sister's head with the TV remote!

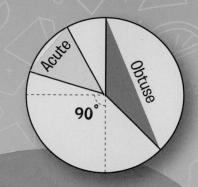

An angle less than 90 degrees is called acute; more than 90° but less than 180° is obtuse, and between 180° and 360° is a reflex angle.

HOLE IN ONE

How can you hit a golf ball from the green so that it goes around the galleon and into the hole? You need to make use of angles, shown by the red arrows. The angle at which the ball hits the kerb will be the angle it bounces off, taking you around the obstacle. It's the same when you're trying to pot a pool ball; the angles hitting the side cushion and bouncing off again are both the same.

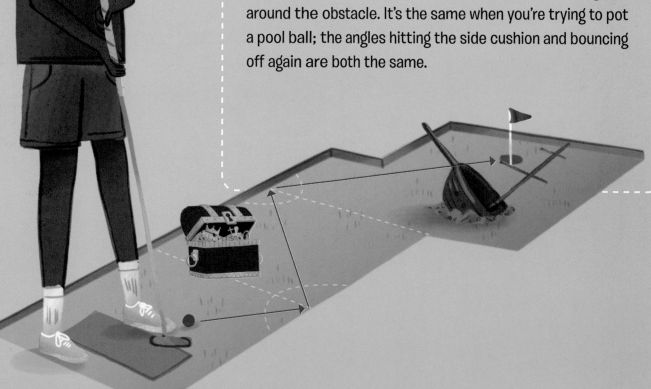

ON REFLECTION

Light behaves in the same way as a ball, where angles are concerned. The light rays bounce off a mirror at exactly the same angle as they approach it. You can use this knowledge to change channel on the TV or even look around a corner! That's how a simple periscope works. Johannes Gutenberg, inventor of a revolutionary printing press, made such a periscope in the 1430s to see over the heads of crowds!

VARYING DEGREES

A full turn back to the starting point takes you through 360 degrees. A half turn, which is a straight angle, is 180 degrees, while a quarter turn gives you a right angle of 90 degrees. Any piece of paper can give you a right angle, even if the edges aren't straight. Fold the paper in half and then fold it again the opposite way. Unfold it to see four right angles.

180°

360°   90°

Shaping Up

Polygons are 2D shapes with straight sides. Their sides meet at points called vertices or corners. There are all sorts of polygons, but we tend to think most often of regular ones, like the honeycomb shape of a hexagon.

ALL TOGETHER NOW

Some shapes fit together in a repeating pattern called a tessellation. Triangles, squares, and hexagons fit beautifully on their own to form regular tessellations. That is because their interior angles divide exactly into 360 degrees. Other shapes need to be mixed together, or to use irregular polygons, to fit without gaps. Tiling patterns like this are seen all around us, in nature, in buildings, and in textiles.

Woo-oo! Irregular shapes can tessellate too!

Inaccurate soccer ball pattern

THE NAME GAME

A regular polygon has all sides and angles the same. They are named according to the number of sides—for example, tri = 3, giving us triangle. Here are the others, up to 10 sides —quadrilateral, pentagon, hexagon, heptagon, octagon, nonagon, decagon. Irregular polygons (which can still be any of the above) have one or more unequal sides or angles, but they must still have straight sides that form a closed shape without crossing each other.

actual soccer ball pattern

There are several "special" quadrilaterals—parallelogram, rhombus, rectangle, square, trapezium/trapezoid, and kite. Their angles always add up to 360.

IMPOSSIBLE PATTERNS

The Dutch artist M.C. Escher was fascinated by tessellating shapes and impossible patterns (see page 118). The soccer ball icon shown on some road signs is an inaccurate pattern, too. The image is made up of hexagons, which works on a flat surface but is mathematically impossible on a curved ball. If you study an actual ball, it uses a mixture of hexagons and pentagons to fit together properly.

The shape of the universe

The universe is full of 3-dimensional (3D) shapes such as cones, cylinders, cubes, and spheres. The mathematical name for some of these is polyhedron. Like polygons, they come in regular and irregular forms. There are only five regular polyhedrons, and the Ancient Greeks thought they were the building blocks of the universe.

triangular pyramid

cube

diamond

Polyhedrons don't have curved surfaces, so cones, cylinders, and spheres are not polyhedrons.

ELEMENTARY

A regular polyhedron is made of faces that are all a regular 2-dimensional (2D) shape, and has all side lengths the same. The smallest one is a pyramid with a triangular base. The Greek philosopher Plato (*c.*428 BCE–*c.*348 BCE) linked this shape to fire, one of the basic elements said to explain how the world and the universe worked. The next 3D shape, the cube, with 6 square faces, is such a neat and strong shape that Plato associated it to the element earth.

Universe = dodecahedron

Fire = triangular Pyramid

THREE MORE

Earth = cube

An octahedron is two square-based pyramids placed base to base, much like a natural diamond. The Greeks linked this smooth-sliding shape to the air. Their fourth element, water, is seen in the beautiful, droplet-like icosahedron, made of twenty triangles. The fifth and final shape is made of 12 pentagons, and is called a dodecahedron. As the Greeks had only four elements, they decided that this last polyhedron must reveal the shape of the whole universe.

Water = icosahedron

icosahedron

dodecahedron

Air = diamond

PRISMS AND PYRAMIDS

A prism has a constant cross section—both its ends are the same shape, and if you slice it parallel to the ends, you get the same shape too. Imagine drawing a polygon and then extending it up in a column from your paper. You have made a prism! You can even push it off to one side, and as long as both ends are parallel, it is a prism. A pyramid is a 3D shape with sloping sides that meet at a point. The sides are triangles, but the base can have any number of edges. The more edges it has, the closer it gets to becoming a cone.

Pyramids are strong shapes for building with, and many ancient examples have remained standing through earthquakes.

A slice of Pi

Pi is the ratio between the circumference of a circle (the measurement around the edge of the circle) and its diameter (the distance across the circle, passing through the middle). It is often written using the Greek symbol π.

Pi has its own celebration day! It takes place, of course, on 3/14 (March 14).

PI IN THE SKY

Pi is NOT an easy number to work out. It is what is known as an irrational number, and is astonishing in its complexity. The decimal digits of pi never end, and although there are only 10 digits to use, they never repeat in a predictable pattern. It can't be shown as a common fraction. The closest we get to showing it as a fraction is 22/7, and it is often written simply as 3.14 for ease.

If you want to remember the first digits of pi, make up a sentence with words containing the corresponding number of letters, such as "How I wish I could calculate pi wisely" (= 3.1415926).

WHAT IS IT?

Circumference

Diameter

Radius

Pi is the circumference of a circle divided by its diameter. No matter how big the circle, the ratio stays the same. If the diameter is doubled, the circumference also gets twice as big. Pi also allows us to work out the area of a circle. Divide the diameter in half (which gives the radius of the circle). The square of the radius (r^2) multiplied by pi tells us the area.

$$\frac{\text{Circumference}}{\text{Diameter}} = \pi = 3.14159 \ldots$$

In 2006, Akira Haraguchi recited 100,000 digits of pi from memory near Tokyo, Japan. It took him 16 hours and 30 minutes!

LOOK, NO CALCULATOR!

Way back in 200 BCE, the great mathematician Archimedes tried to work out pi. He began by drawing a circle and giving it a diameter of 1. He drew squares outside and inside the circle, working out that their perimeters were 4 and 2.8. The circle's circumference was clearly in between those two values. He tried with a pentagon and got two more values that narrowed the value of pi again. He continued until he reached a 96-sided shape, and an estimate of pi that was between 3.1408 and 3.1428. Impressive, huh?

Throwing a curveball

What shape is made when a ball is kicked in the air? Or sliced through its middle? Or when an object is sent into orbit? They are all related shapes, and they can all be made by slicing through a cone.

CONICAL SECTIONS

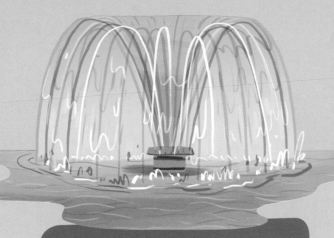

There are four ways to cut a cone to get the different sorts of curves shown in the cross-section. A straight horizontal cut gives us a circle. An angled cut results in an ellipse. A cut parallel with the side of the cone gives a parabola, and a steep angled cut through two cones tip to tip gives a hyperbola.

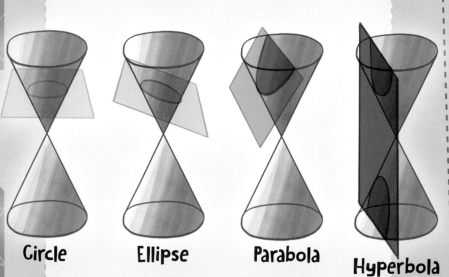

Circle   Ellipse   Parabola   Hyperbola

CIRCLING THE SUN

Earth circles the Sun every year, right? Well, not exactly. Its path is an ellipse, not a circle. Objects in orbit nearly always follow an elliptical path—the Moon around the Earth, Jupiter around the Sun, the ISS around the Earth all have varying degrees of eccentricity (or "squashed-ness"), depending on gravity, distance, speed, and other variables.

The closest point a satellite comes to Earth is called its perigee. Its furthest point is called its apogee. For planets, the related terms are perihelion and aphelion.

TAKE A LOOK

One of the properties of a circle is that all points around it are the same distance from the middle. Measure your bicycle spokes if you want to be sure! An ellipse looks like a squashed circle. Tilt a glass of juice and look down on the surface. It makes an ellipse. Parabolas are curves, such as those formed by water squirting from a fountain, or by kicking a ball into the air and watching it fall. And you will see a hyperbola formed in the light and shadow that a table lamp makes on a wall.

Hyperbola

The famous golden arches of a certain fast food chain are parabolic.

Strong Shapes

Two-dimensional shapes can be built into three-dimensional structures—houses, skyscrapers, towers, and bridges. Some shapes are stronger, while others are economical in their use of materials. Take a look at the buildings around you to see what shapes are visible.

WONDER WALLS

In the 1940s, an American architect named Richard "Bucky" Fuller saw the potential of piecing together triangles (and sometimes hexagons) to make dome-shaped buildings. These "geodesic domes" are extremely strong and use less material than other shapes. A dome-shaped research station at the South Pole was opened in 1975 as a temporary structure and was still providing shelter from extreme weather 35 years later.

STAYING STRONG

Triangles are often used for building, as they are extremely strong. Once the sides of a symmetrical triangle are in place, the angles are fixed and cannot be adjusted in the way that the angles of a rectangle or pentagon can. Triangular structures can hold a lot of weight and withstand strong forces such as wind or earth tremors. From the Egyptian pyramids, built 4,000 years ago, to the Eiffel Tower, built at the end of the nineteenth century, buildings based on triangles can be seen all over the world.

Adding a diagonal to a rectangle, making it into two triangles, makes the weak shape much stronger.

ARCH RIVALS

Polygons aren't the only shapes used in architecture. Arches also appear frequently, beginning many centuries ago. An arch-shaped bridge holds much more weight, and can span greater distances, than a straight, flat bridge. Arch-shaped supports can hold up a roof, or form a window frame, and have been used with great success since Roman times. Some Roman arched bridges and aqueducts are still standing today, 2,000 years later.

Brain bending

When is a donut not a donut? When it's a coffee cup! As jokes go, you might not see the funny side, but this mathematical joke is all about topology. That's the bending, twisting, and distorting of shapes into new shapes, sometimes known as "rubber sheet" geometry.

TWISTED!

Topology is all about stretching and manipulating an imaginary rubber sheet into different shapes. It can be squished up or twisted around, but not torn, cut, or glued. Mathematicians put objects into topological categories according to how many holes go through them. That's what links the donut (a hole in the middle) and the cup (a hole in the handle), so to a topologist, a donut and a coffee cup are no different!

A pot with two handles is topologically equivalent to a pair of scissors, as both have two holes going through them.

TAKING A WALK

The Swiss mathematician Leonard Euler tackled one of the earliest problems in topography way back in the 1700s. In Königsberg, seven bridges linked two islands to the rest of the city. Could Euler plan a tour through the city crossing each bridge exactly once? Euler drew a diagram to show that it can't be done. His drawing represented the links between the bridges, but did not worry about distances and lengths or even the shapes involved.

It is possible to make a 3D shape with only one side! It's known as a Möbius strip and is fascinating. (See more on page 42.)

HOLEY MOLEY!

In topology, a circle is the equivalent of an ellipse (or oval) as it can be turned into it just by stretching it. It is also the same as the c-shape drawn on the board above, as it can be tweaked into that shape. Each shape has an inside and an outside. The c-shape, and the spirals alongside, are all equivalents, and are known as Jordan curves, named after French mathematician Camille Jordan (1838–1922).

IT'S A CLASSIC

The Möbius strip is one of the most famous and most fascinating (and most fun) pieces of mathematics you can play with.

In a twist

To make your own Möbius strip, cut a strip that is 2–3 cm (1 in) wide and 20–25 cm (8–10 in) from the long side of a sheet of paper. Make it into a loop but before you join the ends, twist one end through 180 degrees. Now tape the ends together.

A bug's life

Imagine an ant crawling around the strip. If it were a normal loop, the ant could walk and walk and never reach the end ... but it wouldn't reach every part of the loop. So, if there was honey on the inside, and the ant walked along the outside, it would never get to the honey. On the other hand, if an ant walked around your Möbius strip, it would reach every point on the strip. No matter where you put the honey, it would eventually get to it. Try it with a pen. Draw a line along the middle of the strip. It will cover the entire strip before coming back to the start point. Even better—use scissors to carefully cut along the line you have drawn. See what happens? You don't end up with two separate loops, but one really big one.

Now for something extra freaky and fabulous. Make another strip and cut around it only one third from the edge. Prepare yourself for a shock (and two connected loops)!

THE MEASURE OF THINGS

You can use anything you like to measure things. An item can be as long as a piece of string, as heavy as your schoolbag, or as tall as your dad, but to have true worth and meaning you need to be able to compare your measurements with other people's. Standard units are used around the world to do exactly that; although we sometimes mix it up a little, by using different scales for exactly the same thing.

Some measurements have changed over time, and time in itself has been broken into different parts by different people. We have lost time and altered time, but there is one thing that all scientists agree on—measuring is never a waste of time!

It should take you less than a moment to read this text. Based on a medieval unit of time, a moment is roughly 90 seconds ... although this changed from season to season, depending on how long it took the shadow to move on a sundial.

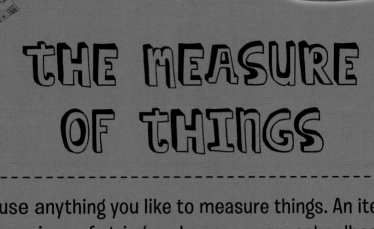

Fancy a date?

time is a difficult thing to measure. Measurements of time are usually based on the motion of the Sun, the Earth, and the Moon, but different cultures have used different astronomical events, giving us different calendars around the world.

the length of the Mayan Tzolk'in calendar is nine cycles of the Moon, and the length of time a pregnant woman carries her baby.

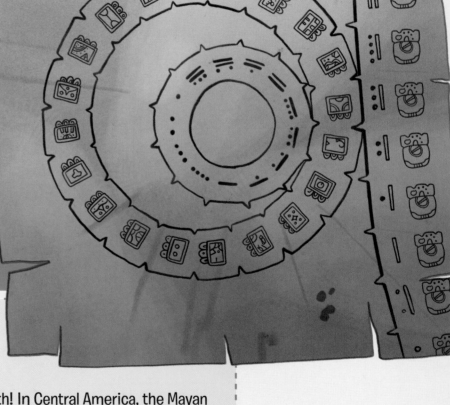

ROUND AND ROUND

The early Islamic calendar focused on the orbit of the Moon, while the Christian calendar used the Sun. The Chinese and Hebrew calendars used both! In Central America, the Mayan calendar dates back over 25 centuries and combines their in-depth knowledge of mathematics and astronomy. It has three wheels or cycles. One of these divides a year into 18 months with 20 days each, plus a final month of just 5 days. Another, the Tzolk'in, splits time into 20 cycles of 13 days, each with its own name and picture.

MODERN DAYS

The Roman emperor Julius Caesar changed the Western calendar in 45 BCE. Before then, a year (usually) had 355 days in it. The Julian calendar divided a year into 365 days, which is the time it takes for the Earth to orbit the Sun. However, the Earth actually takes 365¼ days, and so every fourth year, an extra day was added to account for the spare ¼. Even then, the math didn't quite work properly. The actual orbit time is 11 minutes less than 365¼ days, which added up to a considerable amount over the years. When the Gregorian calendar was introduced in 1582, it was decided that years that are divisible by 100, but not by 400, do not contain a leap day, so 1900 did not have one, and 2100 will not have one, but 2000 did have a leap day.

Before the introduction of the Julian calendar, some years had 378 days, while 46 BCE had 445 days in it!

WORLD TIME

Pope Gregory XIII introduced his own calendar in October 1582 to set things right. The Gregorian calendar is the most widely used calendar in the world today. It wasn't adopted in all countries at the same time, though. Britain didn't change until 1752, and when it did swap, it had to jump from 2 September to 14 September to catch up with the rest of Europe. Sweden and Finland followed a year later, and much of Eastern Europe waited until the 1900s. Turkey switched last, in 1926.

Clock watching

In ancient times, the most obvious ways to describe the passing of time was to use darkness and light, and the movement of the stars and the Sun. There are problems with this system, though! A sun dial is not much use on a cloudy day or indoors, and you can't see the stars on a cloudy night. The timing of day and night also changes throughout the year.

The hands on a modern clock move "clockwise" to imitate the way the shadow moves on a sundial.

SUMMER TIME

Our 24-hour clock comes from the Ancient Egyptians, who divided the daytime into 10 hour-long periods which they measured with shadow clocks. They added one hour at the start and the end for twilight, and divided the remaining 12 hours of night according to the movements of the stars. They changed the lengths of the hours according to the season, so that in summer the daytime hours were longer than night-time hours.

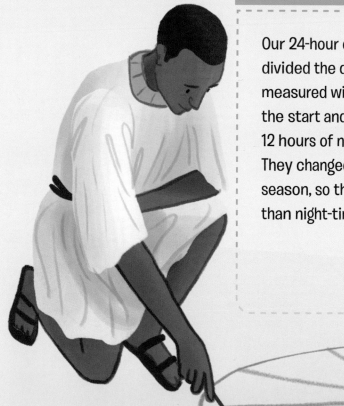

FOLLOW THE LIGHT

People used to know the night sky much better than most of us do today. By finding the North Star (in the northern hemisphere), which holds its position in the night sky, people could check the position of other moving stars and judge how much time had gone by. Similarly, they built sun dials that used the position of the Sun in the sky to cast shadows that show what time of day it is.

The eighteenth-century scientist Carl Linnaeus suggested planting a garden clock that showed the time based on when certain flowers opened and closed their petals.

TIME TRICKLING AWAY

Some early clocks were used to show how much time had passed, rather than what time of day it was. The Chinese used marked candles from the sixth century. Evenly spaced notches were marked in the wax, or on a ruled line behind the candle. Water clocks are even older. They work in a similar way to a sand timer or hourglass, by allowing a regular flow of water or sand from one container to another.

A rule of thumb

Imagine you want to describe how big your new phone is, or the trophy you just won. You could compare them to your outstretched hand to give a good idea of their size. For many centuries, the human body was the natural method used for measuring.

LEND A HAND

Using body parts still lingers in some units today. A horse's height is measured in hands—the distance across the palm and thumb, with the fingers closed. One hand was agreed as a standard four inches by King Henry VIII of England in 1540. Talking of King Henrys, Henry I of England decreed that the distance from his nose to the thumb of his extended arm was one yard (just over 90 cm or 35 in). Try it on your own body!

A person's thigh bone is usually one quarter of their height.

The Egyptian royals also used their arms. the tip of the middle finger to the bottom of the elbow was a cubit (around 50 cm or 20 in).

BODY TALK

Of course, measuring with the body allows lots of room for error. Your tall friend may have longer arms and bigger feet than you. However, the human body shows very interesting ratios, no matter what size you are. For example, the distance between your left middle finger and right middle finger, with arms outstretched, will be extremely close to your height. And the span of your hand from thumb tip to pinky tip is half a cubit (see above).

MEASURE FOR MEASURE

If you have to run a mile, try to make it a Roman one. Theirs was shorter than the modern mile! It was made up of 1,000 paces, or "*mille passum*" with each pace being two steps (roughly 1.5 m or 5 ft). These days, a mile is an extra 56 paces! Maybe the most variable measurement, though, was the perch or rod from fifth-century Saxon Britain. It was defined as "the total length of the left feet of the first 16 men to leave church on Sunday morning!"

Made to measure

In order to compare measurements, everyone needs to use the same system. The height of your new trophy may be three times the length of your hands, but if you order a display cabinet from someone with much smaller hands, it might not fit! That's why we use standard units such as the metric and imperial systems.

SWAP AND CHANGE

The metric system (km, m, cm, l, ml, etc.) is the most common worldwide. However, many of us happily switch between metric and imperial (feet, inches, and ounces), depending on what is being discussed. Athletes compete in the 100m and 1,500m, wherever they are. It is common to refer to a 6-foot-tall person, a 10-mile journey, or a 15-inch laptop screen. And hungry people can order a foot-long sub sandwich, even in a metric country such as Canada or the UK.

The first decimal system was proposed in France in 1670 by an abbot/scientist named Gabriel Mouton.

BUILD IT UP

The metric system begins with a base unit; for example, the kilogram, used to measure mass, and then other units stem from this. The beauty of the metric system is that these other units are all based on powers of ten, so a gram is one-thousandth of a kilogram. Their names give clues as to their size—the prefix "kilo" is Greek for "thousand," while "milli" is Latin for "thousandth," and "cent" is Latin for "hundredth."

In 2013, Myanmar announced that it was preparing to switch from the imperial system, leaving Liberia and the US as the only non-metric countries in the world.

THE POWER OF TEN

A base-10 system makes it straightforward to convert from one level to another. All you do is multiply or divide by powers of 10 (shifting the decimal point). 2 × 1,000 = 2,000, so we know that 2m = 2,000mm, and 200 ÷ 100 = 2, so we know that 200cm = 2m. Imperial measurements are much less logical, with 12 inches in a foot, 8 pints in a gallon, and 16 ounces in a pound!

The unit of length was named from the Greek word *metron* meaning "a measure" and was adopted in 1791.

All around the world

How do you calculate the distance around the Earth without walking it? You could drive, or use satellites to work it out, but long ago neither of those was possible. How about figuring it out using sticks and shadows?

WELL, WELL!

That's exactly what Greek mathematician Eratosthenes did over 2,000 years ago. He knew that on the longest day of the year the Sun was directly over a well at a place called Syene in Egypt. On the same day, he stuck a stick in the ground at his home in Alexandria, about 500 miles away. The stick cast a shadow which allowed him to measure the angle of the Sun there. Using the angles and distances, he worked out the distance around the whole Earth.

Eratosthenes knew that the Sun was directly overhead because its rays shone straight down without touching the sides of the well.

NUMBER CRUNCHING

How did Eratosthenes work it out? He calculated the angle of the Sun to be 7.2° off the vertical. Then he worked out that this is 1/50 of a circle (the Earth's circumference). By multiplying his 500-mile distance by 50, he worked out that the total distance around the Earth was 25,000 miles. He was only around 100 miles over in his calculation; not bad across such a large distance!

MORE OR LESS CORRECT ...

Some historians believe that Eratosthenes may have been less accurate than reported. His distance of 500 miles was an average based on distances given to him by several traders who made the journey regularly. He used the "stadion" as his unit of measurement, but an Egyptian stadion was shorter than a Greek stadion. As we've seen before, it's tricky to compare things accurately if you don't have a standard unit.

Eratosthenes is also credited with being the first person to work out the angle at which Earth's axis is tilted.

Seeing stars

As we venture farther into space, some measurements become useless. The distances involved are so large that miles are meaningless (even the Moon, which is comparatively close, is 384,400 km/238,855 miles away). Instead, we use the term light years to describe the vast distances in space.

Our closest galaxy, the Andromeda galaxy, is 2.3 million light years away (21 quintillion km!).

TALKING TRILLIONS

A light year is, literally, the distance that light can travel in one year. We can only calculate how far this is by knowing how fast light travels, which was first measured in 1676 by the Danish astronomer Ole Rømer while studying Jupiter's moons. The speed of light in a vacuum (space is a vacuum) is 299,792,458 m/s (186,000 miles/s). As there are 31,536,000 seconds in one year, light travels about 10 trillion km (nearly 6 trillion miles) in that time.

WAIT A MINUTE

Radio waves are a kind of light wave and so also travel at light speed. It takes these waves about 1.3 seconds to get to the Moon, which caused a delay when scientists at NASA were communicating with their astronauts on the Apollo missions of the 1960s and 70s. Every time they asked a question, they had to wait about 3 seconds before they got a reply. If we could put people on Mars, it would take between 6 minutes and 42 minutes to hear back from any astronauts there!

It takes just under 8½ minutes for light to reach us from the Sun.

TOO BIG!

Light years are actually too big for our solar system. Our planet is only 150 million km (93 million mi) from the Sun, which is 0.00001582 light years. Just a stone's throw! The closest planet to the Sun, Mercury, is roughly a third that distance. Astronomers use the average distance between Earth and the Sun for these measurements, and they call it the astronomical unit (AU). So Mercury is about 1/3 of an AU from the Sun, and Neptune is around 30 AU away.

Pushing it

How do we measure how hot or cold we are, or the temperature of the air around us? Changes in energy at different temperatures affect the amount of space something takes up (its volume) and can be shown on a thermometer.

MOVING UP

Most substances expand when they get warmer, as their particles have more energy and move around more. A thermometer is a thin glass tube filled with liquid, which is forced up the tube as it expands. It moves up at such a rate that it shows 1 more degree on the scale for 1 more degree in temperature. To be able to compare readings, scientists had to come up with a standard scale. As with so many other measurements, there are still different units in use around the world.

Rising ocean temperatures are making the water expand and rise, causing flooding at the coasts of many countries.

TWO TEMPERATURES

In 1724, Gabriel Fahrenheit gave his name to a scale with 180 degrees between melting ice (32°F) and boiling water (212°F). Around 1743, Anders Celsius (left) used the same base points to make a scale where ice melts at 0°C and boils at 100°C. (Although at first he had them in reverse, with boiling point at 0°C.) Both of these scales drop below zero when it gets really cold, which can be confusing—which is colder, minus 3°C or minus 4°C?

NO NEGATIVES

Negative numbers are not only confusing for the general public; they can make calculations more complicated. In 1848, Lord Kelvin introduced a scale that measures the extremes of hot and cold. Its lowest point is "absolute zero," which is the theoretical coldest temperature where all atoms stop moving. The Kelvin scale has no negative temperatures. Water freezes at 273 Kelvin and boils at 373 Kelvin.

The only temperature where Celsius and Fahrenheit are the same is minus 40 degrees. Very, very cold.

Show me the money

Early people exchanged goods when they needed something (so, for example, an animal skin might be exchanged for a useful tool). This is one of the roles that money plays today—as a way of exchanging things fairly and for an agreed value.

SWAP SHOP

Before money was invented, people used the barter system. They exchanged goods (such as skins or food) or services (fixing your roof or digging your field). However, not everyone needs another animal skin, so something that was valuable for everyone could be used instead. That's where money came in. Precious metals were made into coins that could be handed over for anything you needed, and then spent again by the person who received them.

SAVING AND STORING

Money works as a store of value. You can save up money and it will still be valuable in the future. Imagine if you were given apples instead of pocket money. You couldn't save them because they would eventually rot. You might not be able to spend them quickly if no one wanted apples at that time. Coins and notes are much more practical and long-term.

A lot of early coins were made with a hole in the middle so they could be threaded onto a string.

VALUE FOR MONEY

Money's main use is for exchanging things without bartering. It also helps to measure the value of goods and services. You know that a loaf of bread is worth more than one apple but less than a laptop. Putting a price on these things helps a fair trade between the buyer and seller without having a long conversation every time you want to buy something. It's a lot easier than trying to agree how many apples equals the same as a laptop!

Money can change value over time because of inflation or deflation.

5,500 4,700 5000 apples = 1 laptop

It's a classic

This classic money problem will really boggle your brain at first!

Space café

Three aliens eat at a café. Their meal costs 25 spacebits but none of them has any change, so they put in 10 spacebits each. They tell the waiter to keep 2 spacebits as a tip, so he keeps 2 spacebits from their 5 spacebits change and gives them back 1 spacebits each. Each alien paid 10 spacebits, and got 1 spacebits change, meaning they paid 27 spacebits altogether. The waiter got 2 spacebits, making 29 spacebits total. So where did the missing spacebit go??!!!

Food for thought

The problem with this problem is the way that it is worded means that it all seems correct, but the adding up is inherently wrong. The 27 spacebits INCLUDES the waiter's tip and, from that point on, it all goes wrong ...

It is really easy to explain if you just look at it from the right direction:

- The bill is 25 spacebits
- The waiter gets another 2 spacebits (= 27 spacebits paid to the café)
- Each alien gets 1 spacebit back (= 3 spacebits in their pockets)
- 27 spacebits + 3 spacebits = 30 spacebits altogether

There is no missing spacebit!

TRENDING NOW

Numbers can be gathered together to give us data. This data tells us all sorts of things! A school will keep track of its students' grades. A supermarket will have data about what people are buying. A streaming service will have numbers that tell it what people like to watch. What are people talking, texting, and posting about online? Our every move can be plotted as data and studied as statistics.

Statisticians look for patterns, growth rates, and links to other data. They answer questions about people's habits, but also about weather, disasters, diseases, and other natural events. Their findings are presented as averages and percentages, in graphs, charts, and tables. These allow us to look back over what has happened, and make predictions into the future.

Collecting data is BIG business. And it is growing all the time. It is estimated that by 2020, about 1.7 megabytes of new information will be created for each person on the planet EVERY SECOND. The amount of data is so large it is measured in zettabytes—the name for a trillion gigabytes.

Parts of a whole

Statistics is the science of collecting, presenting, and understanding data. It allows us to get information from numbers. Statisticians often work out things as "parts of the whole" and show them as fractions, decimals, and percentages.

KEEPING COUNT

People have been interested in statistics for centuries. Ancient rulers carried out surveys to keep track of their people, money, and major events such as the flooding of the Nile, wars, and plagues. The oldest census data in existence is from second-century China, which counted nearly 59.6 million people in over 12 million households. Today, we use statistics to work out where to spend taxes, to tell traffic lights when to change, and cure diseases.

Statistics can help us to understand how people live. In China, 35% of all people work in agriculture—compared to just 2.5% in the US.

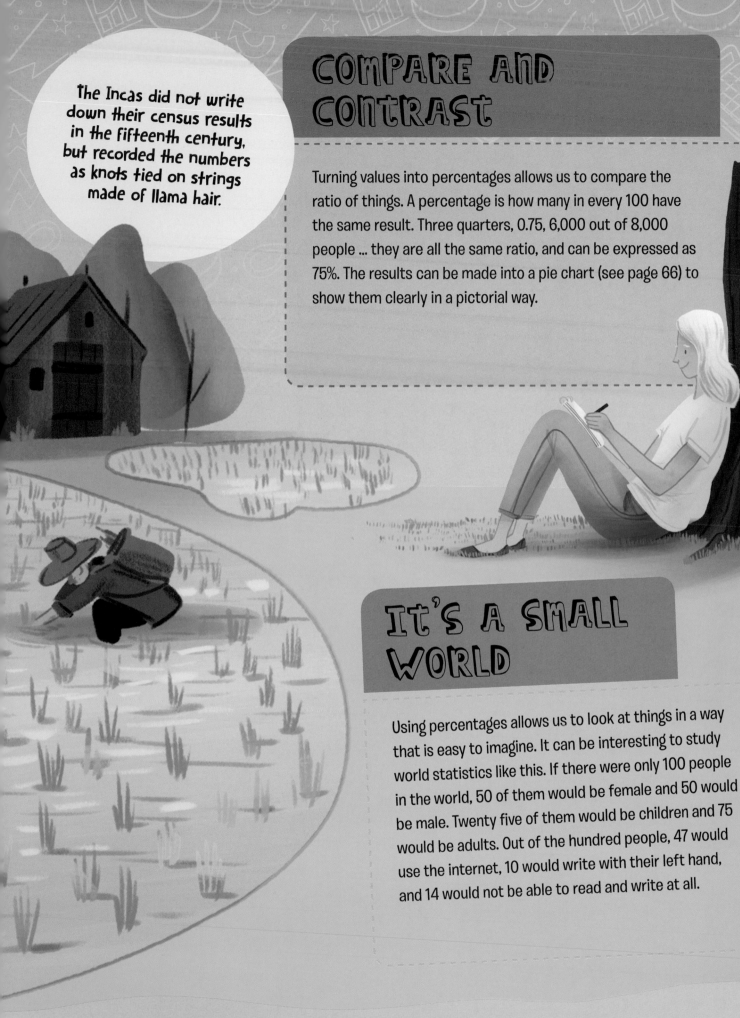

The Incas did not write down their census results in the fifteenth century, but recorded the numbers as knots tied on strings made of llama hair.

COMPARE AND CONTRAST

Turning values into percentages allows us to compare the ratio of things. A percentage is how many in every 100 have the same result. Three quarters, 0.75, 6,000 out of 8,000 people ... they are all the same ratio, and can be expressed as 75%. The results can be made into a pie chart (see page 66) to show them clearly in a pictorial way.

IT'S A SMALL WORLD

Using percentages allows us to look at things in a way that is easy to imagine. It can be interesting to study world statistics like this. If there were only 100 people in the world, 50 of them would be female and 50 would be male. Twenty five of them would be children and 75 would be adults. Out of the hundred people, 47 would use the internet, 10 would write with their left hand, and 14 would not be able to read and write at all.

Above average

Finding an average helps you get information from a set of data. An average is a number or value that represents the middle or typical value. But beware—there are different ways to find an average, and they can all give different results!

MEAN AND MODE-Y

The mode is the most common value in a set. So in a group of children aged 15, 14, 12, 15, and 13, the mode is 15, even though it's the largest number. To find the mean average, you must add the values together and then divide by the amount of numbers that there are: 12 + 13 + 14 + 15 + 15 = 69. 69 ÷ 5 = 13.8. The mean is the most common measure of average.

The mode is the only average that can have more than one value. In a school for 11–16–year–olds, the mode could be 12– and 13–year–olds.

The range of a set gives an idea of how spread out the data is. It is the largest value minus the smallest value.

BETTER THAN AVERAGE

The median, as its name suggests, is the middle value if you place them in order. In the same set of children, the median age is 14: 12, 13, 14, 15, 15. If there are two different middle numbers, the median is the mean of those two numbers. So, to find the median of the ages of a different group of children, whose ages are 12, 13, 13, 14, 14, 15, add the two middle numbers (13 + 14) and find the mean (27 ÷ 2), giving a median of 13.5.

YOUR AVERAGE JOE

What would the average person look like? Well ... there is no average person. If we took average height, arm length, head size, hair shade, and so on, we would end up with someone that is probably unique! The US Air Force found this to their cost when, in 1950, they tried to design a cockpit for the average body size. They measured ten physical aspects of thousands of pilots. After finding the averages, not a single pilot fitted all ten averages exactly!

Something in common

Is there a most common digit? If you look at, say, house prices, or house numbers, or population numbers, or the lengths of the world's longest rivers, will one digit appear at the start more than any other?

LOOK IT UP

In 1881, American scientist Simon Newcomb found some interesting patterns, highlighted by the well-worn pages at the front of data books compared to the pages at the back. People were looking up numbers beginning with 1 much, much more than those beginning with 9. Newcomb, followed around 50 years later by an engineer called Frank Benford, found that in many real-life sets of data, the digit 1 will be the most common leading digit, then the digit 2, then 3, and so on. It has since become known as Benford's Law.

Benford is also known for having devised an instrument for measuring how light travels through glass.

BREAKING THE LAW

Many kinds of data follow Benford's Law. River lengths, populations, and the other examples listed in the introduction all feature 1 as the most common starting digit. In fact, the number 1 occurs first about a third of the time. This pattern can be used to spot crimes, from credit card theft to cheating on tax payments. If a set of data doesn't follow Benford's Law, it is worth investigating.

SHOW AND TELL

Frequency in maths is the number of times a particular data value occurs. Frequency tables or tally marks can be used to show information, such as the number of different types of cars you spot on a journey. The tables can then be used to spot patterns, or present data in different ways, using visual aids such as graphs, histograms, pie charts, and scatter charts. It is much easier to understand some data if it is shown in pictorial form.

William Playfair, a Scottish economist, invented several types of diagram, including the bar chart in 1786 and Pie chart in 1801.

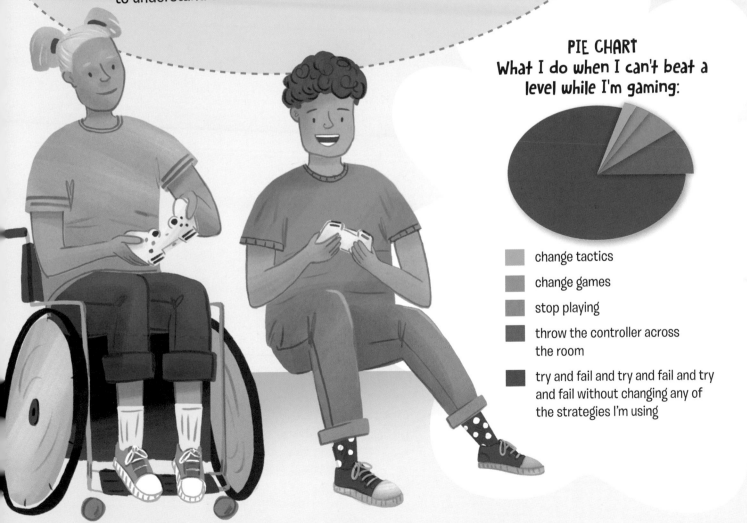

PIE CHART
What I do when I can't beat a level while I'm gaming:

- change tactics
- change games
- stop playing
- throw the controller across the room
- try and fail and try and fail and try and fail without changing any of the strategies I'm using

Double trouble

Some things grow at a constant rate. If you add six football cards to your collection every day, your collection would grow steadily. This is known as linear growth. If, though, you doubled the amount every day, it would grow rapidly and exponentially.

EXPONENTIAL GROWTH

When doubling, numbers get big very quickly. Take a look: 1, 2, 4, 8, 16, 32, 64, 128 ... in 7 doubles we have gone from one- to a three-digit number. If we carry on: 256, 512, 1,024 ... in only 10 steps we have gone from 1 to 1,024. This is known as exponential growth, where a value increases at a rate that is constantly growing. Linear and exponential growth produce very different paths if you plot them on a graph.

Exponential growth helps your savings grow faster. Interest is earned on a larger amount over time, increasing the interest exponentially.

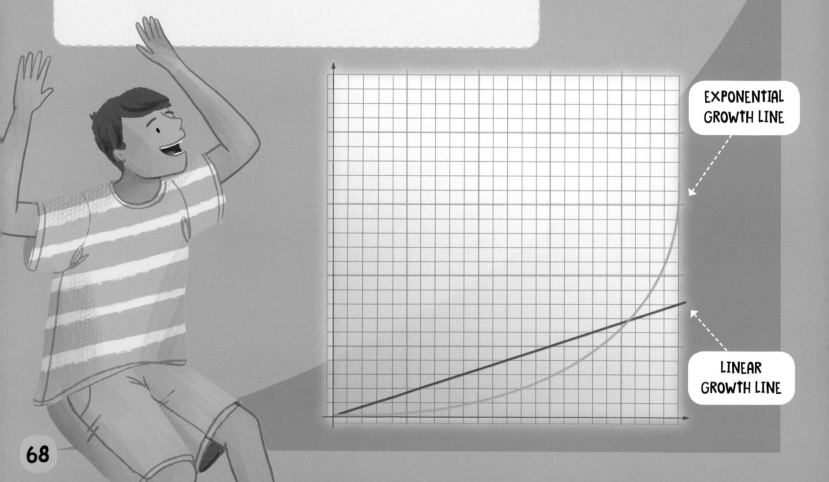

EXPONENTIAL GROWTH LINE

LINEAR GROWTH LINE

RICHER AND RICHER

An ancient tale shows just how large the numbers get when doubling. A wise man won a competition against the king. For his prize, he requested grains of rice: 1 grain on the first square of a chessboard, 2 grains on the second, doubling on each of the 64 squares. The king could not pay. The total prize would have been over 18,000,000,000,000,000,000 grains of rice, which is more rice than there is in the whole world!

Most people think in a linear way, adding instead of doubling. It is harder to imagine how quickly numbers grow exponentially.

TO THE MOON

If you had a piece of paper large enough (and if this was possible) how many times would you need to fold the paper in half to reach the Moon? Theoretically, it would take only 42 folds to get to the Moon. Yes, really! Those 42 folds would make a standard piece of paper (about 0.1 mm thick) into a wedge nearly 440,000 km (273,000 miles) thick. That's easily enough to reach the Moon—which is, on average, 384,000 km (239,000 miles) from Earth.

Looking for links

Two sets of data that are strongly linked are said to have a high correlation. Correlation can be positive or negative, and can be given a value. It can be plotted as points on a chart to see scatter patterns or lines.

HOT STUFF

Let's imagine that you have a year's sales figures for sunscreen. If you were to obtain data on temperatures for that year, you could plot both on a scatter diagram to see if there is a correlation between them. You would expect higher sunscreen sales when the temperatures rose. If one value increases as the other also increases, there is positive correlation. It would show as a line on your chart, rather than randomly scattered points.

Correlation works best looking backward. It tells us for sure what has happened, but cannot accurately predict the future.

C'EST BON!

A correlation between values does not mean that the change in one of them has led to the change in the other. We say that correlation does not equal causation. For example, the number of children getting full marks in a French test increases over a month. It is spring, so the number of sunny days increases over the same period. Does this mean that sunny days cause good French results? No!

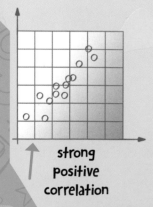

strong
positive
correlation

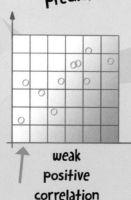

weak
positive
correlation

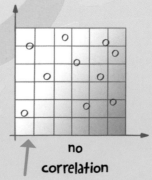

no
correlation

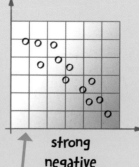

strong
negative
correlation

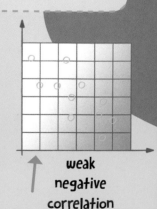

weak
negative
correlation

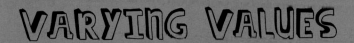
VARYING VALUES

A negative correlation is when one value decreases as the other increases. Think of a birthday cake being shared at a party. If the number of guests increases, the size of each slice decreases. That certainly is a negative effect! A perfect negative correlation shows as a straight line on a scatter chart and has a value of −1. A perfect positive correlation is 1, and 0 is for values that don't seem linked.

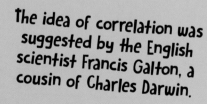

The idea of correlation was suggested by the English scientist Francis Galton, a cousin of Charles Darwin.

Statistically speaking

People can play tricks with information and statistics. Data can be useful, but it can be used in clever ways to suit whatever it is being used to "prove." Statisticians can become magicians and conceal the secrets behind the stats.

DOUBLE COUNTING

Your teacher wants to give you the break time shown on the board. She could announce that she is planning to increase break by 5 minutes every day for the next five days. Or she could tell you that your break time is going to increase by 50 minutes, which is 5 times as much as you have at the moment! Here's how she reaches the 50 minute total: Tuesday increased by 5 minutes from Monday, Wednesday + 10 minutes from Monday, Thursday + 15 minutes from Monday and Friday + 20 minutes from Monday (5 + 10 + 15 + 20 = 50). Clearly, one is more appealing than the other, but is not necessarily an honest way of showing it.

There are so many ways to fudge facts with figures that a whole book entitled *How to Lie with Statistics* was published in 1954.

Monday	10 minutes
Tuesday	15 minutes
Wednesday	20 minutes
Thursday	25 minutes
Friday	30 minutes

A BIT OF A CHEAT

Clever manipulation of numbers can be used to help you. Let's say you score 2% in a spelling test (shame on you!) and then score 3% the next week. Your teacher might comment that your score increased by only 1% and advise you to spend longer revising. But you might tell your parents that your spelling score improved by 50%. Both statements are true, but your cunning plan could save you being grounded!

PLAYING WITH AVERAGES

One common way of disguising information is to use a bar chart where the Y-axis doesn't start at zero. It can make small changes look like much bigger, better changes.

Imagine the school inspector says, "Last year, half of your pupils were below average and they need to improve." But the headteacher says, "Last year half of our pupils performed above average." If they are talking about the median average, then these statements will usually be true, whether it's a good school or a terrible one. If they are talking about the mean average, then it is possible that more than half or less than half could be above average.

Surprise!

Mathematics deals with order, predictability, and right or wrong answers. So how do mathematicians handle surprises and the unpredictable? They use chaos theory. It helps to describe what happens when tiny changes have an effect on the end result.

WHAT HAPPENS NEXT?

Sometimes it is easy to predict how a small change in starting conditions will affect the outcome. If a bus leaves the depot 10 minutes late, it is probably going to arrive at the bus stop 10 minutes late. In other real-life situations, it is almost impossible to make accurate predictions. A ball dropped at the top of a pin board can follow any number of different paths. It will be affected by the speed and direction that the ball is dropped, and how it bounces off each pin.

THE BIG IDEA

Astronomers studying the solar system made many great mathematical and scientific discoveries. Isaac Newton came up with some precise equations that neatly explained the orbit of the planets. However, in the 1900s, a French mathematician called Henri Poincaré noticed that changing the starting point of these orbits, even by tiny amounts, made a huge difference. He had opened up the debate about chaos theory.

The smoke above a blown-out candle is neater lower down. More tiny changes in the air higher up make the smoke swirl and twist.

WEATHER FORECAST

Weather studies are also vulnerable to unpredictable changes. We use mathematical models to try to predict the weather, but it is extremely hard to see a long way ahead. The meteorologist Edward Lorenz found that a tiny decimal error in his computer data had an enormous effect on the results. He wrote about it in 1972, describing it as the butterfly effect—a butterfly flapping its wings may seem unnoticeable, but could be enough to cause a tornado halfway around the world.

Fancy your chances?

Probability is the likelihood that something will (or won't) happen. It can be given a number value: 0 is impossible, 1 is certain, and every fraction or decimal in between shows the chances of something happening.

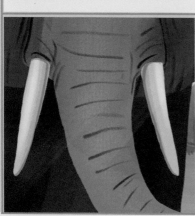

Insurance companies use probabilities to work out their charges. They charge you more if, for example, your house is likely to be damaged by floods or earthquakes.

LOOK, AN ELEPHANT!

Some probabilities are easy to calculate. The chances of your teacher taking a school trip to the Sun are 0. The chances of you breathing in before you finish reading this book are 1. It is unlikely that you will look out of your window and see an elephant, but not impossible. It has a probability greater than 0. A probability closer to 1 shows that something is likely but not definite.

FLIP A COIN

Probability is worked out by dividing the total number of possible outcomes by the number of ways an outcome can happen. If you toss a coin, what are the chances it will show heads? They are 1 out of 2, or a probability of ½. To work out the probability of two or more things happening in a row, we multiply the probabilities together. So, we can write the probability (P) of flipping three heads in a row as: P = ½ x ½ x ½, which equals 0.125 or 1/8.

The sum of the probabilities of all possible outcomes is 1.
For a coin:
P(head) + P(tail) = ½ + ½ = 1.

HEADLINE NEWS

A newspaper ran a story about a family who had three children, all born on the same day of the year, and declared that there was a 48 million to 1 chance of it happening. Except they were wrong. It is surprisingly much, much less than that. They worked it out like this: P(birthday) x P(birthday) x P(birthday) = 1/365 x 1/365 x 1/365 = 48,627,125. But the correct way would be to start with a figure of 1 for the first child, as it doesn't matter what that child's birthday is, as long as the second and third dates coincide. Which gives this: 1 x 1/365 x 1/365 = 133,125, or 133 thousand to 1.

IT'S A CLASSIC

Do you have what it takes to be a millionaire? This classic situation shows exactly how exponential growth does amazing things.

The dilemma

One of our friendly aliens is offered work for a month. She can even choose how she will be paid. Here are her choices:

1. One thousand spacebits every day.

2. An initial wage of 0.01 spacebit, but that wage doubles each day.

3. A single payment of 1 million spacebits.

Which will make her the richest?

Double your money

A wise alien would choose the second option. Here's how much she would earn in 31 days. Take a look at how the money grows. On day 18 she begins to earn more each day than if she chose the first option, and by day 23 she has nearly quadrupled the amount she would have earned with the first option. On day 28 she hits the million-per-day mark, making the third option a poor choice. She still has a few days left to keep doubling her money!

Day	Amount of money	Total so far:
1	0.01	0.01
2	0.02	0.03
3	0.04	0.07
4	0.08	0.15
5	0.16	0.31
6	0.32	0.63
7	0.64	1.27
8	1.28	2.55
9	2.56	5.11
10	5.12	10.23
11	10.24	20.47
12	20.48	40.95
13	40.96	81.91
14	81.92	163.83
15	163.84	327.67
16	327.68	655.35
17	655.36	1310.71
18	1310.72	2621.43
19	2621.44	5242.87
20	5242.88	10 485.75
21	10 485.76	20 971.51
22	20 971.52	41 943.04
23	41 943.04	83 886.07
24	83 886.08	167 772.16
25	167 772.16	335 544.31
26	335 544.32	671 088.63
27	671 088.64	1 342 177.27
28	1 342 177.28	2 684 354.55
29	2 684 354.56	5 368 709.11
30	5 368 709.12	10 737 418.23
31	10 737 418.24	21 474 836.48

TECHNOLOGY

What do chewing gum and the internet have in common?
Apart from being really annoying when they go slow, they both
use technology that wouldn't be possible without numbers.
From bits and bytes and binary in your computer, to black and
white stripes on a gum packet barcode, simple digits
make your world go round.

Technology takes science and mathematics and
puts them to practical purpose. So whether it's putting a
plane in the sky and keeping it there, or letting you talk with
a friend on another continent via a videochat app, it has all
been made possible by mathematicians.

The first pocket calculators only
appeared in the 1970s and cost
nearly US$400. Thanks to advances in
technology, you can now buy one for
less than a tenth of that price, and it
fits in your pocket. Or you can just use
your smartphone ...

Bits of binary

Computers speak their own language. They use binary numbers to store information. Computer programmers may also use something called the hexadecimal system to make binary codes shorter and easier to understand.

10110011001
01100101011001
0011010110011001
01100101011001011
00110010110010101 1
0010011010110

OFF AND ON

A computer works with electrical signals that are either on or off. It's as simple as that. They view everything in this way—is there current, or is there no current? The binary system has only 2 numerals (0 and 1) and so can be used to communicate those ON/OFF pulses. Anything that is processed by your computer, including pictures, music, emails, and games, is represented as strings of 1s (ON) and 0s (OFF) to show different binary numbers.

MICROPROCESSOR

INPUT

One binary digit is known as a bit, and 8 bits makes up 1 byte. Half a byte is known as a nibble!

OUTPUT

COUNTING TO TEN

The decimal system is base ten, and has ten digits: 1 to 9, and 0. Each place in the number represents a different power of 10, which can be put in columns. Every time a number moves one place to the left, it increases by a power of 10 (1, 10, 100, 1000). The binary system is base 2. Each place in the number represents a different power of 2 (1, 2, 4, 8). To convert from binary to decimal, look at a numeral's place and add up the values. Counting to 10 on your hands in base 2 is totally different than counting in base 10!

The hexadecimal system is base 16 and has 16 characters: 0–9 and ABCDEF.

NUMBERS AND LETTERS

Computers don't use the hexadecimal system, but people do, to simplify and shorten binary codes. Hexadecimal (often called hex) allows an 8-bit binary number, such as 11010100, to be written using just two hex digits: D4. It makes it much easier to write long numbers. Hex is often used for error messages and to represent the spectrum of shades made up of red, green, and blue.

From calculator to computer

The history of the computer is a relatively short one, compared to other mathematical discoveries. Inventors had to work out how to make a machine that could not only perform calculations, but could follow instructions to do different tasks.

Babbage designed a Difference Engine, which used only addition, and an Analytical Engine, which had a separate processor and memory store.

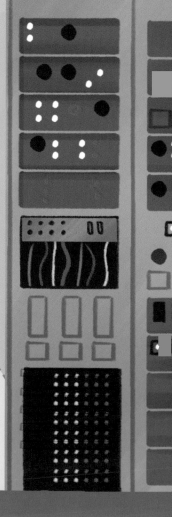

IN THE BEGINNING

The earliest calculating tool we know of was the abacus. It dates back so many centuries that no one is sure where the first one was used. The first mechanical calculating machine was designed by an English professor of mathematics, Charles Babbage. His Analytical Engine of 1837 used punched cards to store numbers in memory units, and was based on the design of a loom used for weaving patterned cloth.

COUNTING ON THE COUNTESS

Babbage's machine was designed to carry out calculations. His fellow mathematician, Ada Lovelace, thought that it could do much more than this. She designed the first computer program—an algorithm designed to be done by a machine (see pages 92-93). She predicted that computers would one day be able to read and manipulate symbols. The Analytical Engine was never actually built before either Babbage or Lovelace died, but it was certainly the building block for computers as we know them.

When she was 12, Ada designed a flying machine. She studied the proportions of birds to help her work out how her machine would work.

COMPUTER GIANTS

The first electronic digital computer was built in 1937. It was called the Atanasoff-Berry Computer (or ABC) after its American designers. It was followed in 1943 by the Colossus computer, designed by British codebreakers at Bletchley Park. The Colossus was hardly a laptop—it weighed 5 tons, contained more than 7 km (4 miles) of wiring, and filled a whole room. It was designed by English telephone engineer Tommy Flowers (shown, left) to crack coded messages in World War II.

Growing but shrinking

Computers have developed rapidly during their short history. In less than a century their processing power has grown from minimal to phenomenal. A smartphone is much more powerful than the computer used for the Moon landing in 1969!

HEADING FOR HOME

The first computers could only solve one problem at a time. They were fed information on punched cards and paper tape, and their output was on printouts. Over time, tiny silicon chips replaced larger parts. These microchips allowed computers to become smaller and faster. The Intel chip arrived in the 1970s and changed everything. What once filled a room could now fit on the palm of your hand. The first computer designed for people to have in their home was launched in 1977.

The first home computers were bought as a kit that you had to put together yourself.

MORE AND MOORE

In April 1965, electrical engineer Gordon Moore wrote that the power of a computer processor would double every year. He updated it in 1975 to what we now know as Moore's Law—that processing power would double every two years. His prediction has been very accurate—though lately the rate has changed to every two-and-a-half years—and is why we've seen such leaps in technology. It has paved the way to things you probably take for granted, from social media and streaming sites to safer cars and cleaner cities.

The Apollo Guidance Computer was more basic than the electronics in some toasters!

OVER THE MOON

The first people walked on the Moon in November 1969. They were guided by computer systems that were no more powerful than a modern pocket calculator. Their Apollo 11 mission used an operating system that allowed the astronauts to control their spacecraft by typing in pairs of nouns and verbs. It had around 64 kilobytes of memory, which is less than 1 percent of the size of the document used to create this chapter of your book!

Under lock and key

As computers have become smaller and more efficient, people now use them for many more tasks. You can order pizza online, pay for it with your phone, and even upload a picture of you eating it, if that's your thing. So how do you keep all your personal info safe?

Experts on computer security predict that cybercrime will cost the world US$6 trillion a year by 2022, a rise from US$3 trillion in 2015.

CHAIN MAIL

In these days of e-commerce and cloud storage, programmers use a tool called encryption to stop other people poking their nose into your business. When you send a message or use the internet, your computer links up with a chain of other computers. A computer-savvy criminal could invade any of these to steal your data. If, however, the information is put into a secret code, the criminal will have to break the code before they get anything useful. Disguising your personal information in code makes it safer.

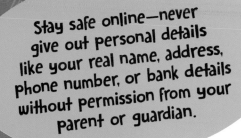

Stay safe online—never give out personal details like your real name, address, phone number, or bank details without permission from your parent or guardian.

SAFETY MEASURES

Think of computer code as if it's a padlock. Information is entered at one end, padlocked up, and then transferred to the other end, where the recipient has the unique key to unlock it. That's where the mathematics comes in. Public-key encryption uses prime numbers as the "keys" to hide a credit card number when you buy online. The customer types in their number and it is encrypted with the seller's public key. It is then sent to the seller, where it is unlocked using the seller's private key.

GIVE ME THE KEY

Why are prime numbers used as the encryption keys at each end of a transaction? It is easy to take two numbers and multiply them together. If the numbers are very large, it is much harder to perform the operation in reverse and find the original two numbers. If they are prime numbers, it is almost impossible to do, even with a computer. Multiply 7901 x 7919. Easy—it is 62568019. It is so much more difficult to start with 62568019 and work out the two prime numbers that multiply together to make it.

Check it out

The barcode was the brainchild of an American inventor named Joe Woodland. He drew his idea in the sand on Miami Beach in 1949, but his black and white stripes on products did not hit the stores until 1974. So, what do all those stripes actually mean?

IT'S THERE IN BLACK AND WHITE

Fact fans may already know that the first ever item to be scanned was a pack of chewing gum. It proved that the info-loaded stripes could be printed on even the smallest of packages. The stripes represent numbers that combine to make a unique combination for each different product. When scanned electronically, they can identify what has been sold, how much it costs, how many are in stock, and when to order new ones.

Barcodes are useful because they still can be read upside down (unlike numbers). They're also clearer—there's no chance of mistaking a 3 for an 8.

BOGUS BARCODES

How does the barcode scanner know whether a barcode is real or not? What if it won't scan, and a wrong number is entered manually? The number that makes up the barcode has a special number at the end that is known as a check digit. It exists purely as a test to see that the barcode has been scanned or inputted correctly. Check digits can also be used to keep credit card numbers and bank account numbers secure against fraud.

BY THE BOOK

There are different ways of generating the check digit. Here is the way that the numbers work to identify different books. A book code (called the ISBN) has 13 digits. Here, the final one has been left off: 978-1-78404-954-__

Step 1: Add the odd digits (i.e. the digits in positions 1, 3, 5, 7, 9, 11, 13): 9 + 8 + 7 + 4 + 4 + 5 = 37

Step 2: Add the even digits (i.e. the digits in positions 2, 4, 6, 8, 10, 12): 7 + 1 + 8 + 0 + 9 + 4 = 29

Step 3: Give the even digits a weighting by multiplying their total by 3: 29 x 3 = 87

Step 4: Add the odd digit total to the weighted even digit total to get an overall total: 37 + 87 = 124

Step 5: The check digit will be the digit needed to add to this overall total to turn it into a multiple of 10. In this case 124 + 6 = 130, so the check digit must be 6.

So, the full ISBN is 978-1-78404-954-6.

Each digit, 0 to 9, can be represented in a barcode with a unique set of vertical stripes.

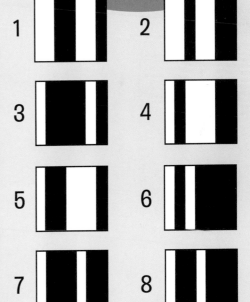

Making Connections

A network is a collection of things that are connected to each other. Mathematicians call the "things" nodes, and map them out on graphs, with connecting lines called edges or links. Networks can represent all sorts of real-life things—the brain, the internet, railways, and even the spread of diseases.

FINDING A WAY

In 1735 Leonard Euler tackled the classic mathematical problem known as The Seven Bridges of Königsberg. Is there a way to walk around the city, crossing each of the seven bridges only once? He redrew the bridges as connections between nodes to make the map into a simple network and show that the walk cannot be done. It was the first example of graph theory.

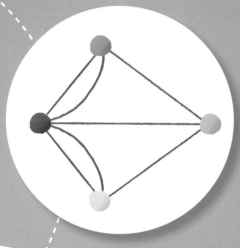

the study of the nodes and connections in networks is called graph theory.

IT'S A SMALL WORLD

In 2009 Ashton Kutcher became the first Twitter account with more than 1 million followers. Now, musicians like Katy Perry and Justin Bieber have more than 100 million.

Many real-life networks have only short distances between the nodes. They are known as small world networks. Social networks, the internet, and our brains are all examples. Nodes that are close together form clusters. You and a friend are two nodes with a link between you. You share lots of friends, who cluster around you. You will probably find that any two people you know are fairly closely linked because of shared hobbies, holidays, or family ties.

SIX DEGREES OF SEPARATION

Stanley Milgram, an American psychologist, decided to investigate social networks in the 1960s. His "small world" experiment tracked chains of people across the United States, asking them to pass on a parcel from the west coast to a specific person on the east coast (picked by the psychologists, but unknown to the initial sender) using only people they knew really well. The parcels got to their destination on average in only six steps! Social networking has rocketed in the twenty-first century, with so many people connected via the internet, on Facebook, Snapchat, Instagram, and Twitter.

Follow the rules

An algorithm is a set of instructions or rules designed to complete a task or solve a problem. It is important that the instructions are written and followed in the correct order or things won't work. Computers need algorithms, but so do you!

GET IT RIGHT

A recipe for baking a cake is an algorithm. The steps must be followed logically and in order for the cake to be baked correctly. It is no good decorating the cake before it goes in the oven! If your friend texts you directions to their house, that's also an algorithm. Many of the processes you use in mathematics are algorithms, following steps in the correct order to calculate the answer to a long division or a quadratic equation.

Algorithms can be used for so many things in computing, from encryption and route planning to internet searches and updating news feeds.

CLEAR AND SIMPLE

Check you have all the ingredients

Go to shop to buy missing ingredients

Preheat oven

Mix ingredients

Put into oven

Bake

Not ready

Ready

Remove from oven

Test with fork to see if it's cooked

Let cool

Decorate

EAT!

Algorithms are the recipe behind computer programming. The ingredients are called inputs, and the step-by-steps are known as the procedure, which eventually lead to outputs. Algorithms are written in English, not in code, and use words like "Start" and "End" to make things absolutely clear. Each step is numbered, and may loop back to previous steps or skip forward, depending on the inputs. Once the algorithm is finalized, it is rewritten in programming language for a computer to understand.

YUM!

SORT IT OUT!

Different algorithms can achieve the same results. If you give someone directions to your school, you could tell them which bus to catch, which streets to drive along, or which shortcuts to take on foot. Programmers have to decide which is the best for their purpose. For example, there are various ways to sort lists (with names like bin sort, quicksort, merge sort, bubble sort), but some are more suited to certain data than others.

Where am I?

It's a question that is easily answered these days if you have a smartphone. But how does your phone know where you are? All it takes is 24 satellites orbiting the Earth, and a bit of mathematical trickery using triangles.

MAP READING

Let's begin on solid ground. In the olden days, if you were lost, you would look for a landmark. Let's say you spot a tower in the distance, and find it on an actual map. You can draw a circle around the tower and know you are somewhere inside that circle. Take another look around; there's a huge hill to your right, roughly the same distance away as the tower. Find it on the map, draw another circle, and your position is one of the two points where the circles cross. If you find a third landmark and draw a third circle, you can tell exactly where you are.

The first global satnav system was set up by the US military, and was made available around the world in 1994.

SEARCHING HIGH AND LOW

Finding your position using three points on a map is called triangulation. Satellite navigation takes it a step further, using trilateration. Each of the satellites beams radio signals toward Earth. If your phone, or any satnav device, can pick up three or four of these signals, it can tell you where you are. It works in three dimensions, not two, so it can even tell you your altitude (how high you are above sea level).

HERE I AM!

Here's how trilateration works. The satellites serve the same purpose as your landmarks (the tower and hill). Except, because the satellites are thousands of miles above your head, and moving, each one pinpoints your position to somewhere within a sphere, not a circle. With signals from three different satellites, the crossover points can narrow your position to somewhere on a circle, and if you pick up a signal from a fourth satellite, you can tell exactly where you are, including your altitude.

IT'S A CLASSIC

You may not be able to make a computer, but you can make your own magic calculator using just numbers on cards.

Magic calculations

Ask a friend to secretly think of a number between 1 and 63 (a whole number, mathematics pedants!). Show her these cards and ask her to point to any that have her number on them. Surprise her by telling her what her number is —wow! (How do you do that? Simply add the number in the top left-hand corner of each card she pointed to.)

How does it work?

The top left-hand numbers are all powers of two ($2^0 = 1$, $2^1 = 2$, $2^2 = 4$ and so on). Any number can be made up of these numbers. Let's say the chosen number is 53. That is $32 + 16 + 4 + 1$. When these cards were designed, all the designer needed to do was to make sure that the number 53 features on the cards with 32, 16, 4, and 1 in the top left corner. Try it for yourself with any other number.

1	3	5	7	9	11	13	15
17	19	21	23	25	27	29	31
33	35	37	39	41	43	45	47
49	51	53	55	57	59	61	63

2	3	6	7	10	11	14	15
18	19	22	23	26	27	30	31
34	35	38	39	42	43	46	47
50	51	54	55	58	59	62	63

4	5	6	7	12	13	14	15
20	21	22	23	28	29	30	31
36	37	38	39	44	45	46	47
52	53	54	55	60	61	62	63

8	9	10	11	12	13	14	15
24	25	26	27	28	29	30	31
40	41	42	43	44	45	46	47
56	57	58	59	60	61	62	63

16	17	18	19	20	21	22	23
24	25	26	27	28	29	30	31
48	49	50	51	52	53	54	55
56	57	58	59	60	61	62	63

32	33	34	35	36	37	38	39
40	41	42	43	44	45	46	47
48	49	50	51	52	53	54	55
56	57	58	59	60	61	62	63

ALL AROUND YOU

Mathematical patterns appeared long before humans thought up or wrote down equations and algorithms. These patterns can be seen in the trees and plants and the insects that pollinate them; they can also be found in spiral snail shells and our fingerprints.

The concepts of symmetry and ratios play a huge part in nature, and in man-made wonders such as beautiful buildings and great works of art. Numbers make harmonious music out of vibrations and notes, and tessellating hexagons help honeybees build their hives. These patterns and repetitions can be seen all around you; it just took special thinkers to find them and figure them out.

Once you begin to notice patterns around you, it can be hard to stop. Check out the bricks in a wall, the symmetry of a butterfly, and the swirling spiral of a hurricane on the news. Patterns are everywhere!

Next, please!

Numbers can form sequences. We can move from one number to the next, then the next, then the next, and see some amazing patterns. It even happens in nature, describing the number of petals on a flower, the number of rabbits born in a colony, and the spirals on a pinecone.

BREEDING LIKE RABBITS

In the Middle Ages, an Italian mathematician called Leonardo of Pisa described a pattern of numbers that is now known as the Fibonacci sequence. The traditional problem asked how many pairs of rabbits there would be after a year, assuming you started with a single pair, and that each pair of adult rabbits (more than 2 months old) produces a new pair of baby rabbits every month. The numbers he found were these: 1, 1, 2, 3, 5, 8, 13, 21, 34, 55, 89, 144 and so on. Look carefully. Each new number is made by adding the previous two numbers together. Here is a diagram showing you the first 5 months–can you draw out the rest of the year?

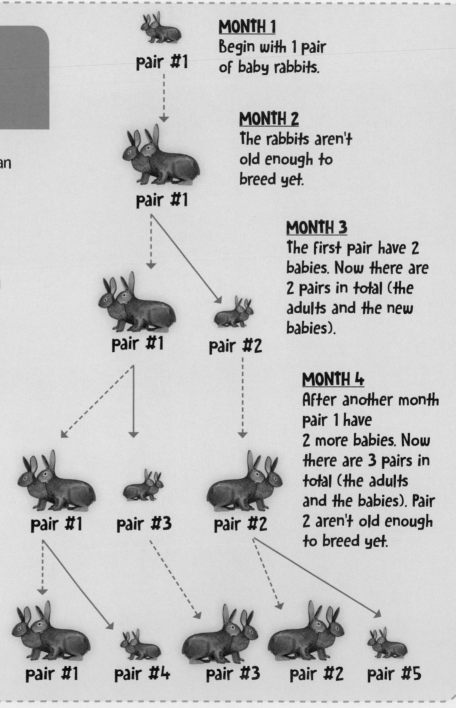

MONTH 1
Begin with 1 pair of baby rabbits.

Pair #1

MONTH 2
The rabbits aren't old enough to breed yet.

Pair #1

MONTH 3
The first pair have 2 babies. Now there are 2 pairs in total (the adults and the new babies).

Pair #1   Pair #2

MONTH 4
After another month pair 1 have 2 more babies. Now there are 3 pairs in total (the adults and the babies). Pair 2 aren't old enough to breed yet.

Pair #1   Pair #3   Pair #2

MONTH 5
Pair 1 and pair 2 have 2 babies each. Now there are 5 pairs in total. Pair 3 aren't old enough to breed yet.

Pair #1   Pair #4   Pair #3   Pair #2   Pair #5

FLOWER POWER

Nature contains all sorts of Fibonacci numbers. Count the petals on flowers. Most will be Fibonacci numbers, even ones with lots of petals, such as daisies. The seeds on a flower head form spiral patterns (as do the sections on a pinecone). Some spiral left and others spiral right, and the number of spirals in each direction is usually a Fibonacci number.

Nature does blip out occasionally, but the averages usually fit the Fibonacci sequence. That's why three-leaf clovers are the norm, and four-leaf clovers are rare.

IT'S ONLY NATURAL

Leaves and branches move in spirals, as they grow, too. It helps them receive the maximum amount of sunlight, and direct as much rain as possible down to the roots. If you study the branching pattern of leaves from their stem, or even the pattern in the veins on the leaves, you will find the Fibonacci sequence. Nature isn't hard-wired with equations, it's just that these numbers form practical or logical patterns that serve nature's purpose.

Leonardo of Pisa went all over the Mediterranean, speaking to traders from lots of places, and learned many mathematical ideas, including the Hindu system for writing numbers instead of Roman numerals.

8
5
3
2
1

Golden time

The Fibonacci sequence is associated with special shapes and relationships between numbers. These are not only found in nature, but also appear a lot in art, architecture, and design. It's all about golden ratios and rectangles.

THE GOLDEN RATIO

The golden ratio is shown by the Greek letter phi (ϕ), and is roughly 1.618. It is an irrational number (like pi) and can't be expressed as a fraction. There is no simple way to put it, so take a deep breath—the golden ratio exists when the ratio between two numbers is equal to the ratio between the total of these numbers divided by the larger number. $(a/b = (a+b)/a = 1.6180339887498948420 ...)$

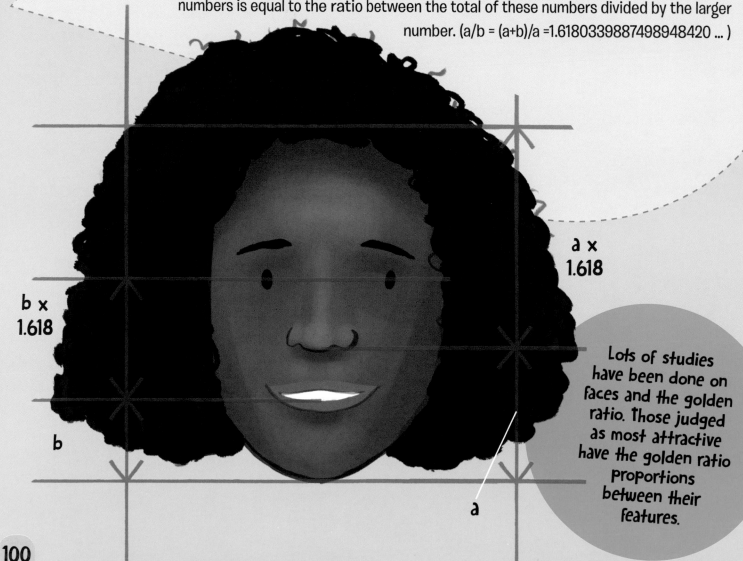

a x 1.618

b x 1.618

b

a

Lots of studies have been done on faces and the golden ratio. Those judged as most attractive have the golden ratio proportions between their features.

GOLDEN RECTANGLES

Draw a rectangle that looks like a picture frame. Now divide the length of the long side by the length of the short side. If your answer is 1.62, the rectangle is golden. It is commonly used in art for its pleasing proportions. Now draw a square inside the frame, with sides the same length as the shorter side of the rectangle. The square and the leftover rectangle have the golden ratio. Golden rectangles are found in all sorts of buildings, from the Great to the Parthenon in Athens and Notre Dame in Paris.

Leonardo da Vinci's painting, the Mona Lisa, shows golden ratios in the position and proportions of the woman's face, body, and clothes.

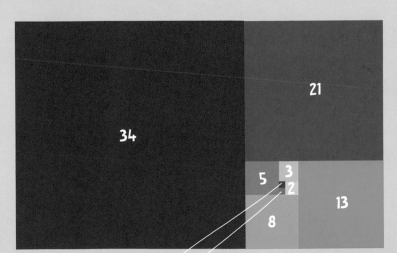

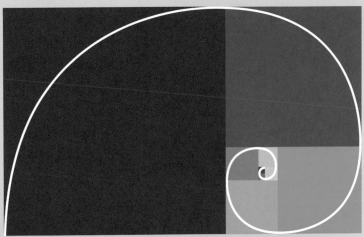

GOLDEN SNAILS

Draw your own golden snail (see pictures above). Start by drawing a square with sides 1 unit long. Keep adding squares in an counterclockwise order with sides following the Fibonacci sequence. Now join the corners of the squares in a smooth spiral. That's a golden spiral, and it can be seen in snail shells, spiderwebs, goat horns, galaxies, hurricanes, your fingerprints, and the inner part of your ear.

Musical musings

Musical notes are named with letters, but music has much more to do with numbers than you might think. There are mathematical relationships between notes that create harmonious sounds, appealing to our logical brains.

HIGHER AND LOWER

If you stretch an elastic band and ping it, it will make a sound. If you use longer or thicker bands, it changes the sound. The Greek mathematician and philosopher Pythagoras (c.570-495 BCE) experimented with strings of different lengths to find out more about this. He discovered that halving the length of a string gave the same note, just one octave higher than the original. He tried doubling the length of a string and got the same note, one octave lower.

MUSICAL DIFFERENCES

Pythagoras didn't use elastic bands, he used a stringed instrument called a lyre. He was interested in the intervals between notes—the relationships between them and whether they sounded harmonious together. When Pythagoras split his string into three, he got a different note from before, but one that still sounded pleasant. He figured out that musical intervals are related to the ratios between string lengths, rather than fixed measurements.

A guitarist shortens the length of the strings (and changes the pitch of the note) by pressing them down with her fingers on the neck (or fretboard) of the guitar.

Sounds are made by vibrations. The number of vibrations per second is known as the frequency of a sound. Halving the length of a string doubles the frequency.

MAKING SWEET MUSIC

Guess what? Fibonacci numbers can be found in music, too. Check out a piano—there are 8 notes in an octave (C, D, E, F, G, A, B, C), which consists of 13 piano keys, split into 8 white keys and 5 black keys, with black keys arranged in a group of 3 and a group of 2. And the golden point of a song or piece of music is usually found at the phi point (see page 100)—61.8% of the way through, rather than in the middle or at the end.

Simple pleasures

A symmetrical shape can be flipped, folded, or turned and will still look the same. It creates a visual harmony, in much the same way that sounds can be harmonious (see page 102). Symmetrical objects play a huge part in the beauty of the world around us.

DRAWING THE LINE

A 2D shape has reflectional symmetry if you can draw a line through it so that both sides of the line match exactly. The line dividing two sides of a shape is, unsurprisingly, called the line of symmetry, and can be vertical, horizontal, or diagonal. Shapes can have more than one line of symmetry. A shape has rotational symmetry if it looks the same when twisted around a midpoint, like a paper windmill. If it looks the same in two positions, it has an order of symmetry of 2.

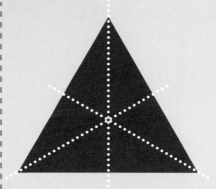

3 lines of symmetry

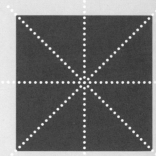

4 lines of symmetry

You can see reflectional symmetry in a mirror, or in a lake reflecting the scenery.

DIVIDED IN TWO

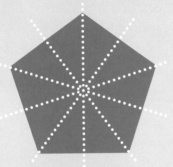

Free-range hens lay more symmetrical eggs than caged battery hens.

Scientists can use symmetry to put living things into categories. Sea anemones, jellyfish, and sea stars have rotational symmetry, as do many flowers and fruits. Most other animals (those with a head and limbs), show reflectional symmetry (biologists call it bilateral symmetry). It is easiest to see in a creature such as a butterfly, but you have it too. A line from your head to your feet would divide you into two similar halves, although some of your internal organs would be on one side or the other.

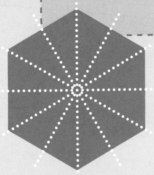

5 lines of symmetry

6 lines of symmetry

PLAYING A PART

Symmetry makes things pleasing to look at, and is important to other creatures in different ways. Scientists have found that male barn swallows with symmetrical tails attract more mates than others, and that bumblebees prefer symmetrical flowers. The bees not only avoided flowers that grew lopsided, but also those where the scientists snipped the petals with scissors. They visited more symmetrical flowers, gathering more nectar and pollinating more of them along the way.

To infinity and beyond

What links CGI, snowflakes, seashells, broccoli, ferns, and Sierpinski triangles? They are all examples of fractals—never-ending patterns that loop and repeat in beautiful, spell-binding ways.

The spiral is one of the most common fractals found in nature.

KEEPING IT REAL

Natural fractals can be tiny or enormous. They are simply patterns that are repeated, from the branches in our blood vessels to the branched patterns of lightning and rivers. Sometimes you can zoom in and find the same shapes repeated forever. A computer can make a fractal pattern using a simple algorithm to repeat the same equation over and over. CGI animation companies use fractals to make things like clouds, fur, hair, and skin look realistic.

REPEATING YOURSELF

See if you understand this mathematics joke—What does the B in Benoit B. Mandelbrot stand for? Benoit B. Mandelbrot!

You can make your own fractal picture. It is called a Sierpinski triangle after a Polish mathematician. Start with a triangle, then shrink it to half its height. Put two identical triangles in the corners below. Repeat that for your new shape, again and again, forever (or until you have to go to bed). The Sierpinski triangle was described in 1915, but the term fractal wasn't used until 1975 when another Polish-born mathematician, Benoit B. Mandelbrot, wrote about repeating shapes in geometry and in nature.

INFINITY IN SHAPES

How can natural shapes be repeated to infinity, within themselves? Think about this. How long is the coast of your country? You could work out the distance on a map, but that doesn't show every twist and turn of the coastline. You could piece together bigger local maps, but even that doesn't include every shape of a field. You could walk the coastline using a trundle wheel, but what if you zoom in even further and measure the distance around each rock that juts out or the curve of every pebble? Where does the measuring stop?

Lost and found

Did you know that mathematics is used to help search for lost objects? It can help people who are looking for ships lost at sea and aircraft lost after takeoff. Computer companies also use it to appear to read your mind and know exactly what you like or might be looking for.

BAYESIAN SEARCH THEORY

Searches use a theory based on Bayesian statistics. This clever bit of mathematics allows us to work out a probability and update it as we go along, using extra evidence. It can be applied to matters of law (how likely is it that a person committed a crime?) and medicine (how likely is a person to contract a disease?). It is especially useful because a search can be given a value—how much will it cost, versus its probability of being successful. When you first start searching for a lost puppy, you should look in the most likely place. When that place has been eliminated (the puppy isn't there), you should check the next-most-likely place. It won't cost you a penny to look under the puppy's most-loved chair, and that's a very likely place he'll be found. However, it's not very likely at all that the puppy is on the Moon, and it would cost a huge amount of money and effort to go check.

The theory was developed in the 1760s by statistician and clergyman Thomas Bayes, but only became widely used from the 1990s.

START THE SEARCH

Here's how it works–the rescue team make suggestions about what might have happened to a lost object (or person, or even a cute dog). They use Bayesian search theory to work out the probability of where the object might be. Their search starts where it is mostly likely to be found, then where finding it is less probable, and so on. Using their calculations, they can carry on until the cost becomes far more than the hope of finding the object.

Search theory was used to look for the remains of Malaysia Airlines Flight 370 that totally disappeared in 2014 on its flight to China.

KNOWING THE MARKET

Computers use the same processes to decide whether an email lands in the junk folder, and to target you with things you probably want to buy. The evidence is weighed up and given probability ratings that determine the outcome. So if an email heading contains WIN WIN WIN, it's likely that it will be classed as spam. If an online company knows that you have bought a dog bed and puppy training pads, the probability is high that you might buy a collar or dog food, and ads will flash up on your screen.

It's only natural

There are so many mathematical wonders and patterns to be found in nature. There are not only symmetry and spirals, but also spots and stripes, meanders and waves, and trees and tessellations. Patterns are recurring shapes, and some of them can be recreated with mathematical models.

A PERFECT FIT

Tessellations fit geometric shapes together with no overlaps or gaps. Nature likes the way hexagons fit together, with 120-degree angles at the meeting point. Honeybees use hexagons to form their honeycombs in an efficient and compact way. It is strong but uses less wax than making it out of tessellating triangles or squares. A fly's compound eye is also made of hexagons, and bubbles form a raft of hexagons when they meet.

Bees use a huge amount of energy to make a small amount of wax. It is thought that a bee needs to eat eight units of honey to produce one unit of wax for building.

PUFFER PATTERNS

Alan Turing, the computer scientist, wrote an article describing how certain mathematical conditions can give living things their patterns of spots, stripes, or blobs.

The tiny pufferfish is a mathematical marvel. Its skin pattern is an example of a Turing pattern made by chemicals. When alarmed, it puffs up into a sphere with a regular arrangement of spikes that stick up. During mating, it creates its own masterpiece of repeating shapes on the ocean floor. The little male uses his fins to dig in the sand, working for days to create giant, symmetrical patterns of ridges and valleys to attract a female.

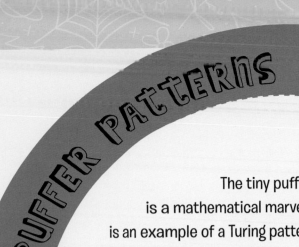

CHAOS AND ORDER

Chaos theory (pages 74–75) is the mathematical study of systems that can be drastically altered by small changes at the start. It explains why streams change their course downhill, splashing off randomly placed rocks as they flow. Mathematicians have studied how it affects fractal patterns (see page 100) to create some of nature's most amazing sights, from clouds and snowflakes to mountains, canyons, and waterfalls.

Getting sucked in

Imagine being sucked into a black hole of endlessly recurring numbers ... AAARGH! But wait! Don't run away. It can't hurt you, it's just a specific type of mathematical magic trick. Let's peer into the void of Kaprekar's constant.

PICK A PIN

Here's the scenario—think of a 4-digit number whose digits are all different. Rearrange them to give the largest and smallest numbers. Subtract the smallest from the largest. For example:

Start number: 5298

Rearrange and subtract: 9852 – 2589 = 7263

Now use this new number to repeat the process ... and again ... and again ... and again, until you end up with the same number on a loop.

5298

9852 – 2589 = 7263
7632 – 2367 = 5265

6552 – 2556 = 3996
9963 – 3699 = 6264
6642 – 2466 = 4176

7641 – 1467 = 6174
7641 – 1467 = 6174

ALWAYS THE SAME

This number (6174) is Kaprekar's constant. Try it again with another starting number of four non-identical digits. (If your answer gives a zero at any point, move it to the far left to get your smallest number, for example 8082 becomes 8820 – 0288.) You will always end up with Kaprekar's constant.

The maximum number of steps before you reach the constant is seven. If your calculations extend beyond that, you have made a mistake!

ERM ... HOW?

For every set of four digits, there is a sequence of numbers that will follow (because the sequence is determined by the digits that you choose). There is one set of four digits that create a subtraction where the largest possible number, the smallest possible number, and the difference between them can all be made from those digits (these are 1, 4, 6, and 7). Once an answer is generated containing these digits, the repetition begins!

This constant is named after the Indian mathematician, D. R. Kaprekar. He was a schoolteacher who simply loved the magic of numbers.

IT'S A CLASSIC

Here's an all-time classic statistics problem from real life. Well, okay, from a TV game shows. It's known as the Monty Hall Problem, after the TV show presenter of the from the 1960s.

Take your pick

Imagine you are a contestant, invited to choose one of three doors. Behind one is the star prize. Behind the others are dud prizes—the classic problem offers goats (baa). You pick door A. Monty Hall checks behind doors B and C and opens one to show you that there's a goat. Now—do you stick with door A, or swap to the other unopened door?

What are the odds?

You would think that eliminating a door leaves you with a 50:50 chance of winning. Odds of 1 in 2 seem better than your original odds of 1 in 3 (when you were guessing blind). You may think that if you switch, you will have a 1 in 2 chance of winning. But surprisingly, switching actually raises your chance of winning to 2 in 3. That's because sticking with your first choice doesn't change the original odds at all. You still have a 1 in 3 chance of winning with this pick. You can't improve this. That means the other door, as yet unrevealed, has the other 2 of the 3 chances. You won't win every time, but the odds have gone up to your advantage. Monty Hall only ever revealed a door that had a goat behind it...

Watch and learn

This puzzle is another example of Bayesian search theory (see pages 108–109). Your chances of finding something improve if you take into account new information as you go along.

HALL OF FAME

What does it take to make your mark on the world of mathematics? Some people shine from an early age, while others take their time before they discover their passion for numbers. Some of the people in this chapter are famous in other fields, from geography to art to nursing, but have still left a legacy in technology, geometry, and statistics.

Travel back in time to find out the famous names of long ago. Some will be familiar, like Pythagoras and his theorem, but others may surprise you. One of the most eminent mathematicians of the fourth century was a woman (three cheers for Hypatia of Alexandria!), while Brahmagupta is the man to thank for nothing—literally, he helped spread the usage of zero. Fast forward through the centuries, and you will find out more about "human computers" and the inventors of actual computing machines. Will your name one day appear in the mathematics Hall of Fame?

Are you in love with geometry? Does algebra make you happy? Follow your heart and choose the subjects you love the most. Many famous names, including M.C. Escher and Florence Nightingale (pictured), have gone against advice from others' to work in an area that they loved, and enjoyed great success.

HYPATIA OF ALEXANDRIA, c.360–415 CE

Famous female mathematicians are vastly outnumbered by males, especially in past centuries. However, there are still lots of women who have made their mark.

Hypatia (*c*. 355–415 CE) was arguably the world's leading mathematician and astronomer of either gender in the fourth century. She was, most unusually, allowed to take an academic role at Alexandria's university, normally offered only to men. Her lectures on all sorts of topics were popular and attracted huge audiences.

Hypatia's father was a great mathematician who taught her astronomy, geometry, and number theory. Her work was not only a continuation of her father's studies, but explored deeper and more technical details. Hypatia's theories on the way the universe works were the most commonly believed for centuries, until Copernicus and Galileo stepped in (in the sixteenth century).

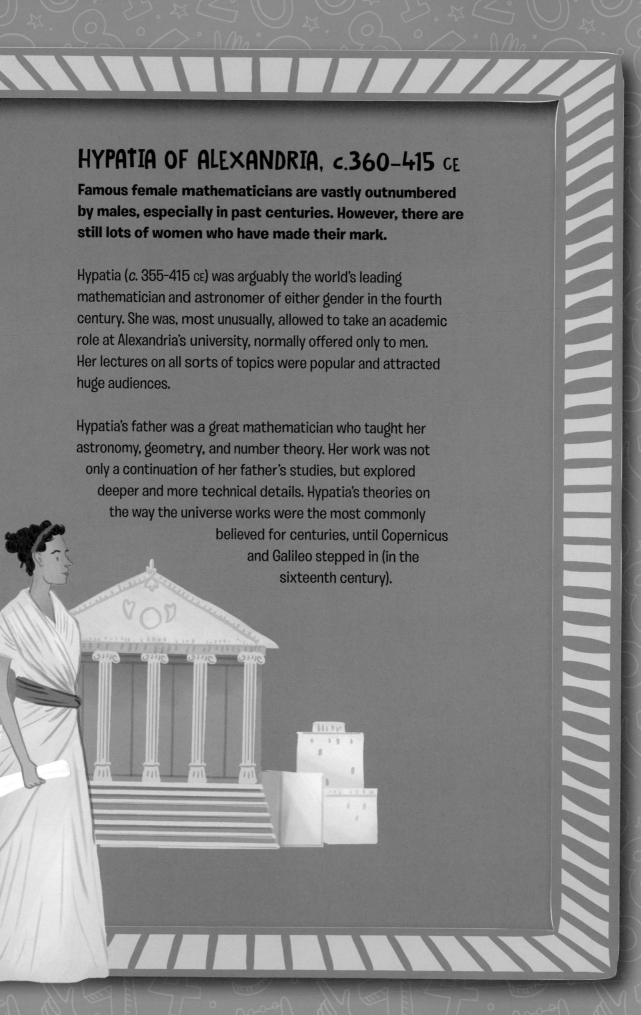

BRAHMAGUPTA, c.598–668 CE

Not many teachers would praise you for zero work, but that's what brought fame to this seventh-century Indian mathematician and astronomer. He was most likely the earliest scholar to write about 0 as a number in its own right. He set down the basic rules for zero that we still accept today: 1 + 0 = 1, 1 - 0 = 1, and 1 x 0 = 0.

Brahmagupta also explained how to deal with squares, square roots, cubes, and cube roots—and showed that numbers could be negative. He demonstrated more rules, for example, a minus number times a minus number gives a positive number. On a grand scale, he opened up the concept of numbers as abstract ideas, instead of them just being for counting and measuring. Unusually, his working out is often missing from his writing, as it was common in Indian mathematics to write down ideas in verse form.

CARL FRIEDRICH GAUSS, 1777–1855

Born in Germany in 1777, Gauss was an astonishing mathematician. At the age of 3, he pointed out a mistake in his father's adding up. Aged 7, he outwitted his teacher by completing a task (adding all the numbers from 1 to 100, according to math folklore) in under a minute.

Despite being poor, his talents were such that a rich duke paid for his further education. Gauss went on to solve 2,000-year-old geometry problems, and recorded 146 ground-breaking math discoveries in his diary. He died in 1855 aged 77, having contributed hugely not only to mathematics but also to astronomy and physics.

M.C. ESCHER, 1898–1972

Maurits Cornelis Escher was an artist, not a mathematician. He claimed to have little mathematical knowledge, and yet his prints and drawings are beautiful and brilliant studies of polyhedrons, tessellation, symmetry, perspective, and abstract notions such as infinity.

Born and raised in the Netherlands, Escher failed his high school exams and dropped out of architecture studies to become a graphic artist. He was fascinated by repeating shapes and filled five notebooks with sketches of all sorts of shapes that fitted together to cover the page. He cleverly interlocked shapes as complex as birds, lizards, and fish. Escher also produced some amazing drawings of impossible spaces and things—staircases that go up and down and never end, water that flows upward, and 2D shapes and buildings that look 3D but could not exist in reality. He also illustrated a Möbius strip with ants crawling along its single edge and single side (see page 42).

PLATO, c.427–347 BCE

Best known as a philosopher, Plato saw mathematics as a way of understanding more about the world. He felt strongly that geometry could reveal the secrets of the universe. When he founded an Academy (a kind of early school) in Athens in 387 BCE he placed a sign above the door saying "Let no one ignorant of geometry enter here."

Plato encouraged all of his philosophy students to study mathematics as well, and taught them how to use simple tools such as a compass and a straight edge. He believed that to be truly educated, scholars had to study the disciplines of arithmetic, geometry, astronomy, and harmonics. He has become associated with setting the Three Classical Problems—namely, squaring the circle, doubling the cube, and trisecting the angle.

PYTHAGORAS, c.570–495 BCE

Born in about 570 BCE in Samos, Greece, Pythagoras was a famous philosopher (thinker) who was interested in mathematical problems. He absolutely loved numbers, and believed they had their own characteristics and strengths. Number 10, for example, was the most complete number because it was made of the first four numbers (1 + 2 + 3 + 4) and formed a triangle when shown as dots.

Several people from different countries studied the geometry of triangles before Pythagoras, but his name is given to one of the most important theorems. It is this— for a right-angled triangle, the square of the longest side (called the hypotenuse) always equals the square of the other two sides added together. The relationship between these measurements can be applied to different shapes, and is used today in all sorts of areas, from map making to computer programming.

Pythagoras was also a musician, and saw important links between mathematics and music.

GALILEO GALILEI, 1564–1642

Galileo was immensely clever. He was known not only for his work in mathematics but also for his work in astronomy, philosophy, engineering, and physics. His contributions to science are enormous, and several had their basis in mathematics.

For instance, in 1581, 17-year-old Galileo, while bored at church, watched a lamp swinging in the breeze. Using his pulse as a timer (because watches hadn't been invented), Galileo timed how long each swing lasted. No matter how far the lamp moved, each swing took exactly the same time. Fascinated by this, he experimented at home with a pendulum. He saw that lengthening the string changed the time, and a pattern of square numbers emerged—to double the time of a swing, the string had to be 4 times longer. To triple the time, the string had to be 9 times longer.

Galileo designed a clock that was controlled by a pendulum, but it wasn't made until after he had died. For more than 300 years afterward, people all over the world used clocks and watches that were regulated by a pendulum or similar.

LUCA PACIOLI c.1447–1517

This Italian mathematician was a religious friar and a friend of Leonardo da Vinci. He has become known as the "father of accounting and book-keeping" for his breakthrough system in balancing money accounts. He wrote about a method used by merchants in Venice with columns for debits and credits. The same method, called double-entry book-keeping, has been used ever since with very few changes.

Pacioli lived for a while in Milan with Leonardo da Vinci. Pacioli taught him mathematics and they worked together on a book about chess.

Friar Luca taught mathematics and wrote textbooks for his students. In one of them, he also explained how to juggle, eat fire, and do magic tricks! His book *De divina proportione*, published in 1509, has illustrations by Leonardo da Vinci. It deals with the application of geometry, perspective, and golden ratios in art and architecture.

ERATOSTHENES c.276–194 BCE

This Greek scholar was a great mathematician, but he was also a poet, astronomer, and music theorist, and he literally invented geography. Wow! He lived in Cyrene, a city that is now in modern-day Libya.

Eratosthenes was the first person to calculate the size of the Earth and the tilt of its axis. He also drew a map of the world featuring parallel lines (similar to modern longitude and latitude lines), and was probably the first person to determine our distance from the Sun. Eratosthenes' sieve is one of the best ways to work out prime numbers, and he invented the armillary sphere to calculate the position of objects in the universe. He was the typical jack of all trades and master of none, though—his nickname "Beta" meant "second-best."

ADA LOVELACE, 1815–1852

Ada was the daughter of Lord Byron, but never knew her father. He was a poet and lived an unconventional life. Ada's mother was determined that her daughter would follow a different path, so she encouraged her to study mathematics and science instead of the arts (which were more traditional for females at that time).

Lovelace worked closely with her friend, the British mathematician Charles Babbage, on his Analytical Engine. It was she who persuaded him that it could be far more than just a calculating machine. She saw its potential to follow algorithmic instructions, like an early computer program, to work out sequences such as Bernoulli numbers. Although her instructions were never tested on a working machine, she has become known as the first ever computer programmer.

BENJAMIN BANNEKER, 1731–1806

Born in Maryland, Banneker was a free black man living in a time when many African Americans worked as slaves. Banneker was self-educated in astronomy and mathematics, and as a young man he invented a carved wooden clock that remained accurate for several decades. He based it on a pocket watch that he had borrowed, dismantled, and made drawings of its working parts.

In his spare time, Banneker corresponded by letter with various mathematicians, setting and solving problems just for fun.

In 1772, Banneker caused a stir, when he successfully forecast a 1789 solar eclipse. His correct prediction contradicted the predictions of better-known mathematicians and astronomers. Banneker had an amazing memory. When the architect on a project to lay out a new national capital (Washington D.C.) walked out and took his plans with him, Banneker remembered and redrew them. Between 1792 and 1797 he published his own *Almanac*—a book of statistics, calculations, and science facts that he had learned.

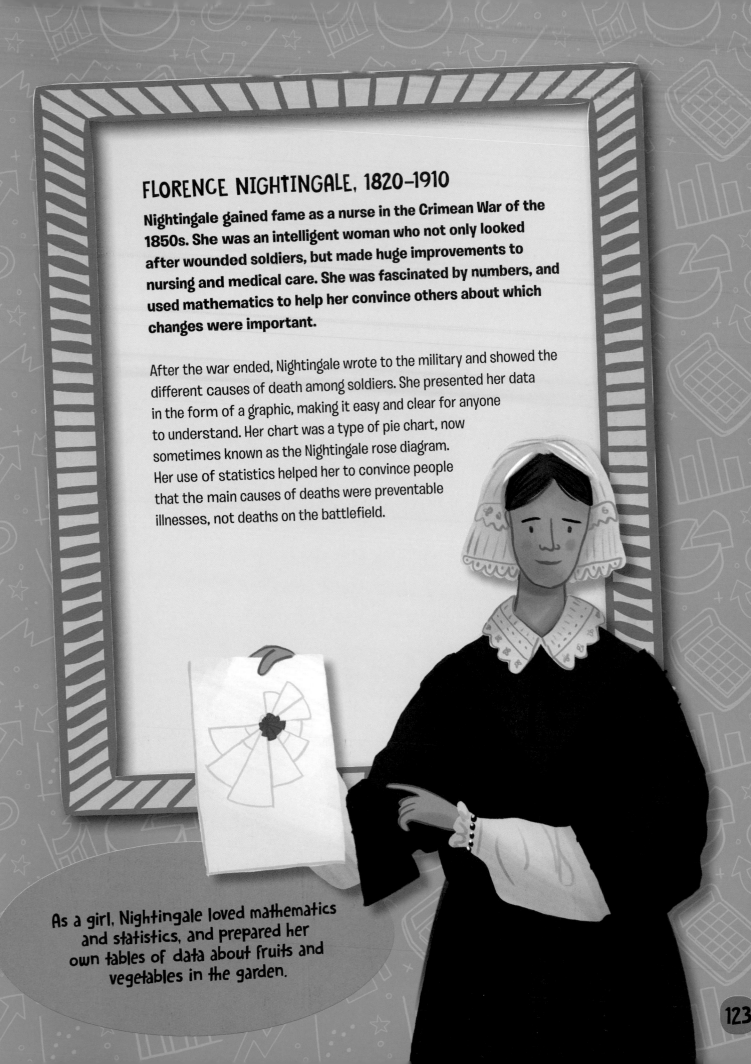

FLORENCE NIGHTINGALE, 1820–1910

Nightingale gained fame as a nurse in the Crimean War of the 1850s. She was an intelligent woman who not only looked after wounded soldiers, but made huge improvements to nursing and medical care. She was fascinated by numbers, and used mathematics to help her convince others about which changes were important.

After the war ended, Nightingale wrote to the military and showed the different causes of death among soldiers. She presented her data in the form of a graphic, making it easy and clear for anyone to understand. Her chart was a type of pie chart, now sometimes known as the Nightingale rose diagram. Her use of statistics helped her to convince people that the main causes of deaths were preventable illnesses, not deaths on the battlefield.

As a girl, Nightingale loved mathematics and statistics, and prepared her own tables of data about fruits and vegetables in the garden.

Turing received an award in 1945 for his achievements with the Enigma Code, but his work at Bletchley Park was kept secret for 30 years!

ALAN TURING, 1912–1954

Turing provides another example of how attitudes have changed. He was a brilliant British mathematician whose work on code breaking during World War II was vital for military intelligence.

Turing was a gifted child, fascinated by science and the practical uses of mathematics. In 1936, he wrote about his idea for a "Universal Machine" that could carry out instructions—the first ever plans for a modern computer. When war broke out, he worked for the government's code-breaking department. Working in a team of mathematicians at Bletchley Park, he invented the Bombe machine for breaking the Germans' Enigma code. After the war, he returned to his development of computers, and also turned his attention to studying Fibonacci numbers in plants and animals. His career was cut short when he was punished for being gay in an age when it was against the law.

GEORG CANTOR, 1845–1918

Cantor was born in 1845 in Russia, but lived and studied in Germany and Switzerland. He was a great thinker, pondering about the theory of numbers, and also arguing about religion and the work of Shakespeare.

Much of Cantor's mathematical work focused on the nature of infinity and sets of numbers (known as Set Theory). He showed that there are different types and sizes of infinity—some numbers are countable, but infinite, while others are simply uncountable. He suffered dreadfully from criticism from older scholars, and was a big supporter of young students later in his life, helping them to put forward their ideas.

DOROTHY JOHNSON VAUGHAN, 1910–2008

Vaughan studied mathematics at university and graduated at the age of 19. She answered an advert looking for African-American women to fill mathematical jobs, which turned out to be a role working for NACA (the forerunner to NASA).

Vaughan joined an extraordinary group of women who carried out calculations for space engineering experiments. The women became known as "human computers" and, because of segregation laws in place at the time, had to work in a separate office from the white people. Vaughan later moved across to NASA's Analysis and Computation division, where she became an expert in computer programming and coding languages. She was part of the team that put America's first satellites into space and sent astronaut John Glenn into orbit in 1962.

You can watch the story of Vaughan and her brilliant colleagues Mary Jackson and Katherine Johnson in the 2016 movie *Hidden Figures*.

FIBONACCI, c.1170–1250

Fibonacci's real name was Leonardo Pisano, and Fibonacci is a nickname meaning "Son of Bonacci" given to him in the 1800s. His father was a wealthy man who took his clever son with him on his travels. Leonardo met many tradesmen and learned a lot from them about arithmetic.

Fibonacci grew up in Italy using the Roman system of numbers (I, V, X, and so on). As he visited new places, he met people who used the Hindu-Arabic system, writing 0 to 9 as we do today. He saw how much easier and faster this was, and spread its usage wherever he could. It took a long time—it wasn't widely adopted throughout Europe until long after his death. His name is given to the famous Fibonacci sequence of numbers (1, 1, 2, 3, 5, 8, 13, 21, 34, 55 ...) that is frequently studied in mathematics.

November 23 is Fibonacci Day, as it has the digits 1, 1, 2, 3. Can you work out the next Fibonacci Day to occur in a year from the Fibonacci sequence?

MUHAMMAD IBN MUSA AL-KHWARIZMI, c.780–850 CE

Al-Khwarizmi is responsible for introducing numbers as we know them into our daily lives. Without him, we wouldn't be counting from 1 to 10 in our early school years. He also brought algebra and algorithms to the western world.

He studied in Baghdad (now the capital of Iraq) in the ninth century and wrote a book called *Hisab al-jabr w'al-muqabala*; the "al jabr" in the title is where the word algebra comes from. The book deals with mathematics such as linear and quadratic equations, but intended for practical purposes. Al-Khwarizmi explains the everyday uses of numbers for things such as buying and selling, measuring land, and building canals. He was also a skilled astronomer and geographer, helping to make maps of the world and work out the distance around the Earth.

SOPHIE GERMAIN, 1776–1831

Mathematics may be all around us, but real life can sometimes get in the way. Sophie Germain found this to be frustratingly true, and the barriers she faced prevented her from becoming one of the great names in mathematical research.

Germain studied the subject from age 13. It's said that the legend of Archimedes sucked her in—he was (supposedly) so engrossed in a geometric shape in the sand that he failed to answer a Roman soldier's question, and was killed for his crime. Germain was intrigued by a subject that was captivating enough to die for, and soon showed natural talent for it. After university, she studied number theory and worked on the notoriously difficult Fermat's Last Theorem, but was often disregarded because she was a woman with less training than the men in her field.

Women weren't allowed to attend university at this time. So Germain enrolled using the name of a male student who had dropped out, and teachers were amazed at the vast improvement in his grades!

GLOSSARY

algebra
Working out equations using letters and symbols to represent numbers.

algorithm
A set of rules to solve a problem

barter
Swapping goods or services instead of exchanging money.

base
How many numbers in a counting system—e.g., Base 2 has 0, 1.

correlation
A link between two sets of data.

cuneiform
A system of writing using wedge-shaped marks in clay.

data
A collection of numbers, measurements, or statistics used for analysis.

decrypt
Decoding a message (see encryption).

dimension
A measurement of length in one direction—e.g., height, width, or depth.

eccentricity
How "squashed" an ellipse is, compared to a circle.

ellipse
A squashed circle, often called an oval.

encrypt
Putting a message or information into code so it is kept private.

exponent
The index or power of a number, for example, the ^{3} in 5^3 (= 5 × 5 × 5).

exponential
Growing in relation to the exponent; the rate of increase gets quicker as the amount gets larger.

factor
Factors are numbers we can multiply together to get another number.

geometry
The area of mathematics that deals with lines, shapes, and space.

infinity
The idea that something goes on and on without ending.

integer
A whole number ie with no fraction or decimal.

polygon
A two-dimensional shape with straight sides.

prime
A positive, whole number that can be divided only by itself and 1.

probability
The chance that something will happen.

symmetry
A shape shows symmetry if it loooks the same after it has been flipped or rotated.

vertex (pl. vertices)
The point where two or more lines meet; a corner.